THE HEART OF HOLINESS

Fr. Gary Lauenstein, C.Ss.R.

THE HEART OF HOLINESS

*Friendship with God
and Others*

IGNATIUS PRESS   SAN FRANCISCO

Cover photograph: iStockphoto.com
Cover design by Riz Boncan Marsella

© 2016 by Ignatius Press, San Francisco
All rights reserved
ISBN 978-1-62164-009-7
Library of Congress Control Number 2014949947
Printed in the United States of America ∞

It is Jesus Christ who teaches us that the heart of holiness is love.

—Pope John Paul II, *The Church in America*

CONTENTS

INTRODUCTION

As in all Catholic religious orders, a man who wishes to become a Redemptorist dedicates a year to an initiation in the spiritual life. Many will tell you that their novitiate year was the best of their life. After all, a novice is given a full year, free from studies, to look at where he is going with his life and to weigh his options.

Unfortunately, I would characterize my year as a Redemptorist novice as the worst year of my life, rather than the best. This was due to deficiencies in me, not in my directors. I did not understand the spiritual life very well. I thought it had to do mainly with rules and regulations. Throughout my novitiate, I had a chip on my shoulder and did not realize it. I felt more and more that God was overly demanding.

For example, there was the dilemma of how seriously I should take the novice rule. We still had in force the rule from a century or so ago that said, for instance, that novices should keep their hands folded across their chest at all times while walking in single file to chapel. And we were told by our novice director that the rule was the voice of God. The conclusion seemed simple: God, through the novitiate rule, was telling us to walk with hands folded across our chest and with eyes demurely cast down to avoid distraction.

But it was the time of the Second Vatican Council. The Church was changing. And every Catholic was uncertain of what those changes meant. What was important in our faith, and what could be dispensed with? None of my fellow novices walked to chapel with his hands folded across his chest. So, for us novices, was the novice rule God's voice or not? More generally, what exactly should we be trying to do when the novice rule told us we should strive for holiness, for "perfection"?

I looked for direction in the writings of Saint Alphonsus Liguori, the founder of the Redemptorists, but self-denial and self-abasement seemed to be his main focus. The process of becoming holy, it seemed, involved mortifications such as fasting and wearing the *cilicium*, the barbed-wire armband that was common in religious orders at that time and was meant to be an irritant, a penance.

Where that was leading caused me a great deal of anxiety and depression. Was I to spend the rest of my life seeking ways to frustrate and irritate myself in the name of penance? I felt trapped, and more than I realized, I was angry. I remember how my anger once subconsciously expressed itself. A new group of novices had arrived to begin their novitiate. I went out to meet them, wearing the cilicium tightly around my bicep and a short-sleeved shirt to make sure the new "recruits" could get a good look at what they were in for. But even in my anxiety, confusion, and anger, I instinctively persevered in prayer, asking only that God guide me to truth.

After our novitiate, my class went to our theology seminary in Oconomowoc, Wisconsin, where we were introduced to undergraduate theology by our professor of Scripture. He proved to hold for me the answer to my prayers.

After he explained to us that the word "gospel" means "good news", I asked him what was so new and good about the Good News? He was happy to tell me. Gradually I came to see that God's love for us is the Good News of Jesus. And with that I had the key for putting things into perspective. I had the key to the spiritual life.

For some years I worked for my province as vocation director, and I found that many of the men who inquired about joining the order had the same questions, even the same anger, as I had in my early years as a Redemptorist. These good men had some knowledge of the externals of penance and discipline, but the heart of those things had not come into focus or been put into perspective in the broader picture of what it means to be loved by God.

The purpose of this book is to help me, and perhaps you, to understand religion as not a mechanical process but a relationship. That means that religion, particularly for a Christian, but also for everyone else, is a form of friendship—with God, with other people, even with one-self. What is true about human friendships is also true about our friendship with God. And what is holy about our friendship with God is instructive to us about our human friendships.

But are my conclusions about the meaning of holiness just my ideas, or have they been part of the thinking of the Church, which has been entrusted with the Good News of Jesus Christ? When I wrote this book, I was privileged to be living at the beginning of the third millennium of the Christian era. I had available to me much of the wisdom of the Catholic Church from the two thousand years of her history, from the New Testament canon to the writings of Pope John Paul II. I found plenty of evidence that the Holy Spirit has been generous in imparting lessons of love to people throughout that time. I therefore include many quotations in support of the notion that the experience of human friendship can teach us how to grow in the friend-ship and love of God. I recognize that many of the quota-tions I offer here are deep and difficult to understand—but only in a quick reading of them. When mulled over in meditation, they yield a rich mine of wisdom.

People who know me might wonder why am I writing a book about the spirituality of friendship. They know that I vacillate between simple neglect of others and infatuation. My only answer can be the same one given by Saint Bernard of Clairvaux, who reformed the Cistercian Order in the twelfth century. He wrote a treatise in which he described the twelve steps by which a soul descends into pride and the twelve steps by which it can climb to humility. For those who might question why he of all people would write about humility, he wrote, "I know more about going down than about going up."[1]

I write here about the kind of friendship with God and others that I would like to have in my life. Unfortunately, I am still working (perhaps not as diligently as I should) on trying to bring these treasures into my life. Perhaps you will find here an echo of your own life's struggles. Perhaps here too you will find some answers to the question "What is holiness?"

---

[1] Bernard of Clairvaux, *On the Steps of Humility and Pride*, in *Bernard of Clairvaux: Selected Works*, trans. G. R. Evans, Classics of Western Spirituality, vol. 56 (New York: Paulist Press, 1987), p. 142.

BEING HOLY MEANS BEING LOVING

What is God like? The apostle John answers this question in his first letter, and I wonder if what he says did not come from his own experience of being the Lord's "beloved disciple", who rested his head on Jesus' chest at the Last Supper (see Jn 13:23). Saint John tells us that in our everyday living, the one experience that helps us to understand God best is the experience of love: "God is love, and he who abides in love abides in God, and God abides in him" (1 Jn 4:16). Thus, the more we understand love, the more we will understand God. And the more we live in love, the more we will live in communion with God.

Saint John Chrysostom was the bishop of Constantinople in the last half of the fourth century and is recognized as one of the *Doctores* (the Latin word for "teacher"), or Doctors, of the Church; that is, his writings can be trusted to promote the genuine and authentic teaching of the Church, a teaching that he himself lived out.[1] His nickname, Chrysostom (Greek for "golden mouthed"), was given to him because he was such an eloquent preacher.

---

[1] B. Forshaw, "Doctor of the Church", in *New Catholic Encyclopedia* (New York: McGraw-Hill Book Company, 1967), 4:938–39.

John Chrysostom tells us that friendship with one another introduces into us the very life of God, the Holy Spirit of love. He says that our love for one another has the result of living in God.[2] Pope John Paul II picked up the same theme: "In his intimate life, God 'is love' (cf. I Jn 4:8, 16)."[3] That means in the inner life of God, the Spirit of love is shared between the Father and the Son and is himself a Person of that Trinity of Persons.

The heart of the mystery of holiness is to realize that we are called to be friends with God. Holiness is not the result of a mechanical process in which grace is coinage and we are given so many graces in return for so many good deeds. Holiness describes a healthy, personal, loving relationship with God as our Friend. According to the bishops of the Second Vatican Council, "Through this revelation therefore, the invisible God (see Col. 1:15; I Tim. 1:17) out of the abundance of His love speaks to men as friends (see Ex. 33:11; Jn. 15:14–15) and lives among them (see Bar 3:38), so that He may invite and take them into fellowship with Himself."[4]

There is an important place for good deeds in our religion. The formula for keeping our practice of religion pure is a simple one: "Religion that is pure and undefiled before God and the Father is this: to visit orphans and widows in their affliction, and to keep oneself unstained from the world" (Jas 1:27). This definition of religion is true because we discover the standard for loving God in our love of other people. And we discover the standard for loving other people in our love of ourselves.

[2] Cf. John Chrysostom, Homily 77, in *Commentary on Saint John the Apostle and Evangelist, Homilies 1–47*, vol. 33 of The Fathers of the Church, trans. Sr. Thomas Aquinas Goggin, S.C.H. (Washington, D.C.: Catholic University of America Press, 1957).

[3] John Paul II, *On the Holy Spirit in the Life of the Church and the World* (*Dominum et Vivificantem*), 10.

[4] Vatican II, Dogmatic Constitution on Divine Revelation (*Dei Verbum*), 2.

The ways of holiness, then, simply reflect the ways of friendship. The more we understand human friendships, the better we will understand the relationship we are called to with our Divine Friend. Either having a good friend or *being* a good friend, even if the attempt is not reciprocated, can teach us a great deal about the relationship God wishes to have with us.

Saint Francis de Sales (1567–1622) was a bishop and a Doctor of the Church who wrote a series of letters of advice to someone he chose to call Philothea, which means "lover of God". Later he was persuaded to gather these letters into a book, which he published as *Introduction to the Devout Life*. De Sales uses the words "devout" and "devotion" as we would use the words "holy" and "holiness". In these letters, therefore, he gives Philothea his insights into what holiness means.

De Sales says that an artist paints all the faces in his works based on the women he has known and loved.

> So too everyone paints devotion according to his own passions and fancies. A man given to fasting thinks himself very devout if he fasts, although his heart may be filled with hatred. Much concerned with sobriety, he doesn't dare to wet his tongue with wine or even water but won't hesitate to drink deep of his neighbor's blood by detraction and calumny. Another man thinks himself devout because he daily recites a vast number of prayers, but after saying them he utters the most disagreeable, arrogant, and harmful words at home and among the neighbors. Another gladly takes a coin out of his purse and gives it to the poor, but he cannot extract kindness from his heart and forgive his enemies. Another forgives his enemies but never pays his creditors unless compelled to do so by force of law.
>
> All these men are usually considered to be devout, but they are by no means such. Saul's servants searched for

David in his house, but Michol [David's wife] had put a
statue on his bed, covered it with David's clothes, and thus
led them to think that it was David himself lying there sick
and sleeping. In the same manner, many persons clothe
themselves with certain outward actions connected with
holy devotion, and the world believes that they are truly
devout and spiritual, whereas they are in fact nothing but
copies and phantoms of devotion. Genuine, living devotion, Philothea, presupposes love of God, and hence it is
simply true love of God.[5]

Saint Alphonsus Liguori, who founded the Redemptorists in 1732 and is also a Doctor of the Church, sums up
the argument his saintly predecessor de Sales makes: "Some,
says Saint Francis de Sales, make perfection consist in an
austere life; others in prayer; others in frequenting the sacraments; others in alms-deeds. But they deceive themselves:
perfection consists in loving God with our whole heart."[6]
Both saints say genuine holiness simply means love for God.
Alphonsus quotes Francis de Sales on this point:

> For my part, I know of no other perfection than that of
> loving God with our whole heart; because all the other
> virtues, without love, are but a mere heap of stones. And
> if we do not perfectly enjoy this holy love, the fault lies
> with us, because we do not, once for all, come to the con-
> clusion of giving up ourselves wholly to God.[7]

The Church's liturgy echoes this conviction. The prayer
for Holy Thursday morning says, "God of infinite compassion, to love you is to be made holy."

[5] Francis de Sales, *Introduction to the Devout Life*, 1, 1.

[6] Alphonsus de Liguori, *The Practice of the Love of Jesus Christ*, in *The Holy Eucharist*, vol. 6 of *The Complete Works of Saint Alphonsus de Liguori: The Ascetical Works*,
ed. Rev. Eugene Grimm, C.Ss.R. (New York: Benziger Brothers, 1887), p. 264.

[7] Ibid., p. 301.

A Definition of Love

Saint Augustine, the prolific Christian writer and bishop who lived from 354 to 430, also a Doctor of the Church, defines "love" as the movement within the soul that would bring it to enjoy God for God's own sake and to enjoy one's self and one's neighbor for God's sake.[8]

It is important to understand that real love is not just an emotion. A "movement of the soul" is a tendency or a direction. Augustine says a loving heart takes flight toward (or seeks to seal a bond with) God. That bonding with God he calls "enjoying God". Since God is all love, all beauty, and all truth, Augustine's definition is not too surprising, because love, beauty, and truth draw us to themselves. But Augustine says we lean toward enjoying God for God's sake rather than our own. And when he says we are to "enjoy ourselves", he means we are to be in communion with ourselves or to be balanced and integrated in our own personality. And we are to enjoy our neighbor, meaning that we are to be in communion with him. Love of ourselves and love of our neighbor ultimately are for God's sake, as is our love of God. Love then is not essentially a feeling. It is the whole direction our life takes toward our being better integrated in ourselves, in communion with others and in communion with God.

Saint Thomas Aquinas, another Doctor of the Church, lived in the thirteenth century. He was a great teacher of theology, yet he has a simpler definition of love: "To love is to will the good of another."[9] His definition is important because it points out that we do not necessarily try always to do what the person we love wants; rather, we try to

---

[8] Cf. Augustine, *Christian Instruction*, 3, 10, 16.
[9] Thomas Aquinas, *Summa Theologica*, I-II, 26, 4.

do what is best for him. Of course, God, who is perfect love, wants what is best for him and us alike. Our feelings of affection for other people, however, sometimes confuse us and lead us to do whatever the other person wants, when in fact it may not be good for him, for us, or for God. And so, doing the person's will in this case is not really love. The Spirit of holiness is also the Spirit of love and of truth. "Love" that is inconsistent with truth is not love.

The Necessity of Love

In his encyclical letter *The Redeemer of Man*, Pope John Paul II wrote, "Man cannot live without love."[10] Saint John Chrysostom says much the same:

> Suppose that a man has no friend—a condition of utter madness—(for the fool will say: "I have no friend" Sir. 20:15); what sort of life will such a man live? Even if he be wealthy ten thousand times over, even if he live in opulence and luxury, even if he be possessed of advantages without number, he is actually destitute and stripped of everything.[11]

I read a newspaper story about a thirteen-year-old boy in Oregon who was placed in a detention home by his parents, who said they could do nothing with the boy. Not long afterward, the boy ran away and took shelter

---

[10]John Paul II, *The Redeemer of Man (Redemptor Hominis)*, 10.

[11]John Chrysostom, Homily 78, in *Commentary on Saint John the Apostle and Evangelist, Homilies 48–88*, vol. 41 of The Fathers of the Church, trans. Sr. Thomas Aquinas Goggin, S.C.H. (New York: Fathers of the Church, 1954), pp. 349–50.

with a group of hobos. Those hobos proved to be very concerned for him and did what they could to take care of him. When he was discovered by the authorities, he was taken away from the hobos and brought back to the detention home. But before long he broke away from that place again and went back to live with the hobos who had shown him honest affection and concern. The story points to a truth we have all experienced: if we cannot find love where we should be able to find it—in our families and among our friends—we will look for it elsewhere.

The *Catechism of the Catholic Church* indicates that our need for love comes from the fact that we are created in God's image, and God is love. So we become more like God as we become more loving: "God who created man out of love also calls him to love—the fundamental and innate vocation of every human being. For man is created in the image and likeness of God who is himself love" (1604).[12]

---

[12] Cf. Gen 1:27; 1 Jn 4:8, 16.

2

FRIENDSHIP WITH OTHERS

Friendship with another person in and of itself is a holy gift. The *Catechism of the Catholic Church* affirms, "Whether it develops between persons of the same or opposite sex, friendship represents a great good for all. It leads to spiritual communion" (2347). The Old Testament book of Sirach describes friendship as a treasure: "A faithful friend is a sturdy shelter: he that has found one has found a treasure" (Sir 6:14).

It is at the same time true that many saints were suspicious of human friendships. They feared that loving another person would distract them from loving God as completely as possible.

So we have something of a dilemma on our hands. We have a natural inclination toward friendship, and we are taught by the Lord to love our neighbor as ourselves. At the same time, great saints have warned us not to allow our love for others to distract us from the love we owe God. A resolution to that dilemma is to purify or consecrate our human friendships so that they will be genuinely helpful. This requires two steps:

1. We should seek out those friends who will share our spiritual values. We will consider this more later, when we talk about sharing values in friendship.

2. We should learn from every human friendship how to be friends with God. After all, holiness, as we have seen, means being friends with God. And so we accept every friendship as a reflection of the kind of friendship God wants to have with us.

What lessons about friendship with God—that is, holiness—can we learn from our friendships with other people? What are the elements of genuine friendship?

Presence to the Friend

An essential element of any friendship is the opportunity for friends to be together frequently. Ralph Waldo Emerson warned that friendships risk dying through long absences: "Go oft to the house of thy friend, for weeds choke the unused path."[1]

The word "comrade" indicates the need for physical presence at the origin of friendship. It comes from the Latin word *camera*, meaning "room." In Spanish it is translated *camara*. When travelers would stay at an inn, they would often stay several to a room, *camarada* in Spanish, perhaps translated colloquially today as "roommates". This word passed to French as *camarade* and to English as "comrade". The English words "chamber" and even "chum" have the same origins.[2]

Those for whom we feel the strongest affection are gifts, blessings from God, because they reveal so much about the nature of love and what genuine, abiding love should be.

[1] Ralph Waldo Emerson (1803–1882) quoted in Transcendentalists, www.trancendentalists.com/emerson_quotes.htm.

[2] Wilfred Funk, *Word Origins and Their Romantic Stories* (New York: Wilfred Funk, 1950), p. 57.

When we feel strong affection for someone, we cannot get enough of his presence. We cherish every moment with him. We feel hollowness in his absence. And we think about him even when he is gone. Such feelings have shown me the importance of spending time with other people. A spiritual director once advised me to spend more time with others. He said that I should make a point to sit with them, to be in their presence. My nature is task oriented and not people oriented. I am more like Martha than like Mary (see Lk 10:38–42). I am always ready to jump up and do something rather than to sit and do nothing but wait with someone. Learning to enjoy sitting idly with some people has made me wish to spend less time on projects and more time with all people.

The Absence of the Friend

When I examine the lessons that feelings of affection teach me in my efforts to grow in genuine love, I see the importance of physical presence. But I also recognize that the physical absence of the friend does not necessarily mean that the friendship has to end. And for religious people there is always the possibility of bearing the absent loved one in mind through prayer.

In the letters of Saint Paul we find many examples of love for those who are absent.

To the Christians in Rome Paul wrote:

> For God is my witness, whom I serve with my spirit in the gospel of his Son, that without ceasing I mention you always in my prayers, asking that somehow by God's will I may now at last succeed in coming to you. (Rom 1:9–10)

To the Corinthians, whom he had had to scold in a previous letter, he said:

> And I wrote as I did, so that when I came I might not suffer pain from those who should have made me rejoice, for I felt sure of all of you, that my joy would be the joy of you all. For I wrote you out of much affliction and anguish of heart and with many tears, not to cause you pain but to let you know the abundant love that I have for you. (2 Cor 2:3–4)

Paul sent one of the Philippians' emissaries back home to them with an observation about that good man's longing for his community:

> I have thought it necessary to send to you Epaphroditus my brother and fellow worker and fellow soldier, and your messenger and minister to my need; for he has been longing for you all, and has been distressed because you heard that he was ill. (Phil 2:25–26)

To his protégé, Timothy:

> Paul, an apostle of Christ Jesus by the will of God according to the promise of the life which is in Christ Jesus, To Timothy, my beloved child: Grace, mercy, and peace from God the Father and Christ Jesus our Lord. I thank God whom I serve with a clear conscience, as did my fathers, when I remember you constantly in my prayers. As I remember your tears, I long night and day to see you, that I may be filled with joy. I am reminded of your sincere faith, a faith that dwelt first in your grandmother Lois and your mother Eunice and now, I am sure, dwells in you. (2 Tim 1:1–5)

Saint John Chrysostom was asked whether his insistence on the importance of friendship was not contradicted by the fact that many thought hermits living by themselves, perhaps on mountaintops, were holy people. Chrysostom answered: "The solitaries surely have many admirers; and these would not admire them if they did not love them. Furthermore, they themselves in turn pray for the whole world, and this is a very great proof of friendship."[3] He was saying that even the most remote hermit has friends in the people whom he bears in mind and in prayer.

The depth of that love we can see in a letter that Saint John Chrysostom wrote to such a hermit friend, Saint Maro:

> We are bound to one another by ties of love and esteem, and I can see you as if you were here: the eyes of love are such that they can penetrate any distance and are not weakened by the passing of the years. I wish I could write to you more often ... but do you write often and tell me how you are.... To know that you are well is a great comfort to me in this wilderness. And above all, don't fail to pray for me.[4]

Grief

Grief plays an important role in the loss of a friend. We would not feel grief at the loss of a friend if we did not first feel love for that friend.

[3]John Chrysostom, Homily 78, in *Commentary on Saint John the Apostle and Evangelist, Homilies 48–88*, vol. 41 of The Fathers of the Church, trans. Sr. Thomas Aquinas Goggin, S.C.H. (New York: Fathers of the Church, 1960), p. 351.

[4]Donald Attwater, *St. John Chrysostom: The Voice of Gold* (Milwaukee: Bruce, 1939), p. 29.

A wealthy Frenchman lost a son in the First World War. He would go each year to the site where his son died, thinking that somehow by being there, he was in contact with him. Even when he was an old man, his limousine would pull up to the side of the road there, and two husky servants would carry him in his wheelchair to the tree where his son died and discreetly leave him alone for a time.[5]

Grief is not a sign of personal weakness; rather, it gives testimony to the strength of love. When we cry because a friend disappears from our life, we are not lesser persons. We are simply persons who love others.

Saint Bernard of Clairvaux was followed into the monastery by his favorite blood brother, Gerard, who served as the steward for the monastery. When Gerard died, Bernard presided over the funeral. He made it through the Mass and the burial without a tear. But a few days later, giving a lecture to his fellow monks on the biblical book the Song of Songs, Bernard broke down:

> How can I be concerned with "The Song of Songs" amid such sorrow? The violence of my pain carries my thoughts elsewhere, and the Lord's indignation dries up my mind.... Until now ... I controlled myself, so that my emotion might not appear to be stronger than my faith.
>
> You know that when everyone else was weeping, I followed the funeral cortege without shedding a tear. Still without shedding a tear, I remained standing by the grave until the end of the funeral. Wearing priestly vestments, I recited for him with my own lips the customary

[5] Gene Smith, "Still Quiet on the Western Front", *American Heritage Magazine* 16, no. 6 (October 1965), www.americanheritage.com/content/still-quiet -western-front.

prayers. According to usage, I threw a little earth with my own hands on the body of my beloved who was about to become earth in his turn!

Although I was able to hold back my tears, I could not overcome my sorrow.... [S]orrow thus stifled has taken deep root and become the more violent in the measure that it was more firmly repressed. I admit myself vanquished, I must give vent to my suffering. I can certainly let it be seen to the eyes of my children![6]

Saint Aelred, another Cistercian abbot in France in the twelfth century, also gave vent to his grief in his funeral oration for a dearly beloved friend named Simon:

For you one should rejoice, yet I should be wept over because I must live without Simon. What a marvel that I be said to be alive when such a great part of my life, so sweet a solace for my pilgrimage, so unique an alleviation for my misery, has been taken away from me. It is as if my body had been eviscerated and my hapless soul rent to pieces. And am I said to be alive? O wretched life, O grievous life, a life without Simon! The patriarch Jacob wept for his son, Joseph wept for his father, holy David wept for his dearest Jonathan. Simon, alone, was all these to me: a son in age, a father in holiness, a friend in charity. Weep, then, poor fellow, for your dearest father, weep for your most loving son, weep for your gentlest friend. Let waterfalls burst from your creased brow, let your eyes shed tears day and night. Weep, I say, not because he was taken up but because you were left.[7]

---

[6] Msgr. Leon Cristiani, *St. Bernard of Clairvaux* (Boston: St. Paul Editions, 1983), pp. 148–49.

[7] Aelred of Rievaulx, *Mirror of Charity*, in *Aelred of Rievaulx: The Way of Friendship*, ed. M. Basil Pennington (Hyde Park, N.Y.: New City Press, 2001), p. 76.

Friends for All Eternity

There is a consolation for Christian hearts (and for many others who believe in eternal life) who have to say good-bye to a friend. Friendship is the one thing that we can "take with us". Friendship endures past death. The friends we have made on earth may remain our friends for all eternity, if we wish to have them as our friends. The one thing that consoles me the most in being separated physically from those for whom I have the strongest affection is the knowledge that these separations are only temporary. Once these friends and I have entered eternity, there will never be cause for us to be separated again. We will be with each other and the Lord Jesus for all eternity. Jesus has assured us: "I am the resurrection and the life; he who believes in me, though he die, yet shall he live, and whoever lives and believes in me shall never die" (Jn 11:25–26).

One of our Redemptorist missionaries told me a story about his family. When he was small, he had two younger brothers. They both caught scarlet fever, and the doctors could not save them. The younger boy, "Buddy", died during the afternoon, while the older boy was fading quickly. His parents would not tell him his brother had died. Suddenly, staring at the upper corner of the room, the boy said a prayer that he was accustomed to say at the Consecration of every Mass: "My Jesus, Lord and God, I adore you, I worship you, I love you." Then, pointing to the same corner, he exclaimed, "Look, there's Buddy!" He died soon after. I'm sure it was Buddy whom he joined in that short walk into God's arms.

So I look forward to being with my friends in that life that is forever. And in the meantime we have the consolation of the Catholic doctrine that we are still in contact with our loved ones who have preceded us in death. The Second Vatican Council's Dogmatic Constitution on the Church said: "But all in various ways and degrees are in communion in the same charity of God and neighbor and all sing the same hymn of glory to our God. For all who are in Christ, having His Spirit, form one Church and cleave together in Him (cf. Eph 4:16)."[8]

Blessed Francis Xavier Seelos was a Redemptorist missionary who came from Germany to work with immigrants in the United States in the nineteenth century. Even though his life as a missionary took him far away from his family, he continued to love them very much. He was especially close to the sister nearest him in age, Antonia.

> In a letter to Father Bernard Beck, June 6, 1872, she writes: "Though he [the Servant of God] loved all his brothers and sisters very much, still, even as a student, he wrote to no one but me, and I entrusted to him all my secrets and matters that were close to my heart." In his farewell letter, December 16, 1842, he says that "Even though I am far away, love remains and unites us eternally, here in prayer for one another, there in a joyful meeting without parting."[9]

When a close friend by the name of Ivo died, Saint Aelred talked about sensing his presence just the same:

> Indeed, the fond memory of my beloved Ivo, yes, his constant love and affection are, in fact, always so fresh to my mind, that though he has gone from this life in body, yet

---

[8] Vatican II, Dogmatic Constitution on the Church (*Lumen Gentium*), 49.

[9] Carl Hoegerl, C.Ss.R., *Documentary Study of the Life, Virtues and Reputation for Holiness of the Servant of God Francis X. Seelos, C.Ss.R.* (Roma: Tipografia Guerra, 1998), p. 150.

to my spirit he seems never to have died at all. For there
he is ever with me. There his devout countenance inspires
me. There his charming eyes smile upon me. There his
happy words have such relish for me that either I seem to
have gone to a better land with him or he seems still to be
dwelling with me here upon earth.[10]

I celebrated the funeral of a man who had been a
very active church member at Holy Redeemer Parish in
Detroit, Michigan. During the months of his dying from
cancer, he met with his family to plan his funeral Mass. He
prepared his family well for his departure. The day after his
Mass, a family member told me that the family had been
startled by an unusual thing. When they came home from
the funeral Mass, they found their lily plant in full bloom.
They took this as a sign from their deceased loved one that
he was safely home in heaven.

When I precede my friends in death, I hope they will
not hesitate to ask for my prayers. I hope that God will give
me some way to assure them of my presence to them, even
when I am absent in body.

Saint Thérèse of Lisieux told her fellow sisters on her
deathbed: "Do not weep, for I shall be more useful to you
after my death and I shall help you then more effectively
than during my life."[11]

Communication with the Friend

If we are to experience friendship at all, we must break out
of our isolation and communicate with others.

[10] Aelred of Rievaulx, *Spiritual Friendship*, in *Aelred of Rievaulx*, p. 73.
[11] *St. Thérèse of Lisieux: Her Last Conversations*, trans. John Clarke (Washington, D.C.: ICS Publications, 1977), p. 102.

I read somewhere the unusual story of a man who was picked up by the police for vagrancy and prowling. He appeared not to know how to talk and would cringe and cry anytime anyone got near him. He knew no sign language. He refused to eat and was beginning to starve to death. Even with no means of communicating with him, the police were able to devise a way to break through his isolation. They brought in another prisoner to eat with him. He followed the prisoner's example, ate, and even asked for more. Communication was established without words and without conversation, first by way of example.

When physical presence to the friend is not possible, at least some form of communication with him or some sort of mutual retention of memories is necessary. A story of extraordinary patience in communication is that of Florence Border and Marjorie Jackson. For fifty years, Florence of Altadena, California, and Marjorie of Manchester, England, corresponded as pen pals. They kept in touch through the Depression and World War II, and the Borders sent food packages to the Jacksons after the war. The Borders, who had no children, also sent packages to the Jacksons' grandchildren. Too poor to travel, neither had met the other. But there was a genuine friendship simply in their efforts to remain in communication with each other.

Conversely, just because the friend is physically present, we should not assume we are growing in our friendship. In fact, unless there is meaningful communication, friendship will tend to die.

Effectively, Abraham Lincoln's family life came second to his career as a lawyer and a politician. For example, when he was a congressman in Washington, D.C., there was nothing he liked more after a grueling day than to come home and sit by the fire to read a book. His wife,

Mary Todd, who had been cooped up with their small children all day, was starving for adult conversation. In such circumstances Abe would tend to ignore her. On one occasion, while he was reading, she told him the fire was going out and he would have to put more logs into the fireplace. He paid no attention. She repeated her request. Again, there was no response from Abe. Finally, she picked up a piece of firewood and whacked the future president of the United States right on the nose.[12]

Mary Todd Lincoln needed more than a hand with the firewood from her husband. She needed communication with him, an acknowledgment of her presence, of her needs, an opportunity to grow with her husband through their conversation.

When the shoe was on the other foot, Abraham Lincoln himself relished being able to have someone listen to him. Dale Carnegie in his book *How to Win Friends and Influence People* gave an example from the life of Lincoln to illustrate one of his (Carnegie's) major principles: that a good conversationalist is a good listener who encourages the other person to talk.[13]

The story he told was that Lincoln had asked an old friend from Springfield, Illinois, to visit him in Washington. When the friend arrived, Lincoln talked for hours about the advisability of making the Emancipation Proclamation. He went through the pros and cons and looked at newspaper articles and letters. Finally, Lincoln thanked his friend for his time and sent him back to Springfield. The friend had not said a word. He had simply listened,

---

[12] David Herbert Donald, *Lincoln* (New York: Simon and Schuster, 1995), p. 108.

[13] Dale Carnegie, *How to Win Friends and Influence People* (New York: Simon and Schuster, 1937), p. 114.

and that seemed to be all that Lincoln really needed from him. Carnegie said that that seems to be all that people often need from us.[14]

On the spiritual plane, conversation can become a marvelous vehicle of grace. Focusing on the other person in conversation helps us move away from self-centeredness. It helps us grow in our appreciation and love of another. As Confucius said, "It is not the failure of others to appreciate your abilities that should trouble you, but rather your failure to appreciate theirs."[15]

The upshot of all I want to say about conversation is that it can be the vehicle for drawing us closer to other people, creating the possibility of friendship. With my closest friends, conversation was a sort of bonding, as if we were extending our hands to each other by means of our words. In such cases I have always felt the desire to continue the conversation. One trip I took with a friend was ten hours long. We talked nearly the whole way. To me it seemed to pass in fifteen minutes. Even though what we discussed was not very significant, I was able to converse with my friend for hours without growing weary of the experience.

Knowing the Friend

Ultimately, the result of conversation with another person is that we get to know him better. Knowledge of a person comes from spending time with him and especially from listening to him. A friendship comes about when we discover that the person whom we desire to know has the same desire to know us.

[14] Ibid., pp. 112–13.
[15] Confucius, *The Analects*.

A hint that another person regards me kindly and lovingly is in his understanding of me. How thrilled I am when someone I care about tells me he feels he has a lot in common with me. As the Indian poet Kabir once put it, "He understands who loves."[16]

Sometimes we have to force understanding on ourselves by presuming goodwill on the part of our friend. Another Indian author tells how one morning his servant failed to show up at the usual time. Doors remained locked; the water was not drawn from the well; his morning meal had not been prepared; his clothes were not set out for him. As the hours passed, the employer's anger grew. His servant was nowhere to be found. Finally, late in the morning, the servant showed up. The employer did not wait for an explanation; rather he told the servant he was fired and that he would be happy never to see him again. "My little daughter died last night", was all the servant could manage to say; then he began his round of daily duties.[17]

We are capable of great understanding toward those for whom we feel great affection and whose affection we in turn value. There is a story to the point about a woman who invited her neighbor to go with her on an outing the next day. "There is someone special you just have to meet," she explained to her neighbor. All that evening the neighbor tried to figure out who the special person was she would meet the next day. The neighbor knew that the woman's husband worked for the symphony orchestra. Could it be they would have lunch with the symphony conductor? Or perhaps there was some special

---

[16]Kabir, in *One Hundred Poems of Kabir*, trans. Rabindranath Tagore (London: Macmillan, 1915), p. 11.

[17]Based on Rabindranath Tagore, quoted in Tony Castle, *More Quotes and Anecdotes* (Northport, N.Y.: Costello Publishing, 1986), p. 262.

soloist coming to town she would be honored to meet. Or it might be some rich and famous patron of the orchestra.

The neighbor was quite surprised to find that the woman took her to a nursing home. She learned that the woman visited there once a week. Instead of the famous person she had imagined, the neighbor met an elderly lady. Through the course of the conversation, the neighbor discovered that the elderly lady had been the mother of twelve children, that one of the children had been handicapped, and that the mother had had to care for that child well into his adult years. And all this after the lady had been widowed early in life.

After the visit in the home, the neighbor was still curious. "Why did you take me out to this home to meet that particular lady?" she asked.

"She has been quite an inspiration to me," the woman who invited her said, "and I want everyone I know to get to know about this remarkable person."

Anyone else seeing the elderly lady dozing off in the lobby of the nursing home might have dismissed her as not very significant. The woman who had come to know her through conversation had a far better understanding of her. And she had grown to love her.

Conversely, we can say that a lack of understanding between individuals is based in a lack of love. Saint Paul constantly urged members of the communities to which he wrote to arrive at some mutual understanding and love: "I entreat Euodia and I entreat Syntyche to agree in the Lord" (Phil 4:2). It is very common in the confessional or in spiritual direction to hear people complain about how difficult it is to live with others in their lives, be it family, coworkers, or fellow religious in a community. It all comes down to the same challenge: Have I come to see these people as friends?

It is true that, as François de La Rochefoucauld tells us, "we always love those who admire *us*; more than those *we* admire."[18] But it's also true that "in admiring greatness we rise to its level."[19] When I list all the good qualities I find in my friends, it is partly to demonstrate my love and admiration for them, but also to remind myself of what I should become.

An especially liberating moment in a relationship comes when I am able to talk with a friend about our relationship itself. When I discover he cherishes the friendship as much as I do, it is a joy. Nevertheless, it is easy to become over-bearing in seeking a relationship.

One priest told me that a woman in the parish he served had taken a liking to him. She sought every opportunity to be with him and to talk with him. Then she began giving him gifts. At about that time, but not for that reason, he was transferred to another parish out of state. The phone calls and letters from her kept coming, and so did the gifts. Finally, exasperated, he told her to cease and desist. She was incensed. She took revenge. For years thereafter she packed the week's garbage in a box and sent it to him.

A relationship can become overbearing and a friendship can be lost if one of the parties in the relationship insists *too much* on talking about the relationship. I wonder if a sign that the relationship may be becoming too intense is found when a sense of humor is lost in the relationship. Perhaps if we are not so serious in our conversation, we will not become overly intense in our relationship. Saint Thomas Aquinas wrote: "It is requisite for the relaxation of the mind that we make use, from time to time, of playful deeds and

[18] *Maximes*, no. 294, in *The Macmillan Book of Proverbs, Maxims, and Famous Phrases*, selected and arranged by Burton Egbert Stevenson (New York: Macmillan, 1948), p. 15.

[19] Cuyler Reynolds, *The Banquet Book* (New York: G.P. Putnam's Sons, 1902), p. 262.

jokes."[20] It's the old story of the bow that remains bent too long and loses its strength. A friendship turned too intensely upon itself becomes too demanding to bear.

Ultimately the goal of growing in knowledge of another person is to determine whether he is as interested in us as we are in him. But forcing another person to declare his feelings about us does not work. A classmate told me a truth he had learned. He picked up a handful of sand and said, "If you squeeze it, it runs out of your hands." And it did, as he showed me. "But if you hold it on your open palm"—he showed me—"it stays with you." True friendship is not possessive. It respects the integrity and the individuality of the other.

So, conversation and communication reveal much to friends about one another. Provided that the self-revelation remains respectful, it can help build up friendship. Saint Augustine commented on Saint Paul's assertion (1 Cor 13:13) that, of all the virtues, the greatest and the one that will last forever is love: "Let knowledge be used as a kind of scaffolding with which to build up love. Love endures forever, even as knowledge fails."[21] He was saying that we have to grow in our knowledge of another before we can hope to grow in true love and devotion. That knowledge includes a realistic assessment of how much our friend wants our affection.

Sharing with the Friend

I have always considered it a privilege to do something for a friend because of my affection for him. Once when a friend went to Mexico, I lent him what was to me at the

---

[20] Thomas Aquinas, *Summa Theologica*, II-II, 168, 2.
[21] Augustine to Januarius, Letter 55, 21, 39.

time a prized possession: my camera. It was not principally because I wanted to see photos of Mexico—though
I was interested in seeing what he would bring back—but
because lending him my camera was another way of telling
him he was important to me. I tried to tell him as much.
I said that if the camera were lost, broken, or stolen, he
should not fret over it. I said he was more important to me
than any camera.

Saint Valerian sets the tone for what sharing with a
friend means. He said that even a small gift can seem great
if it bears the love of the giver.[22]

Mutual Benefit

A friendship is particularly valuable and authentic when it
has some mutual benefit. In the animal world, there are
remarkable examples of such symbiotic relationships. One
of them has to do with the pinna, a type of shellfish that is
blind but is inhabited by the Alphaeus crab. The two work
together. The pinna opens its shell. The crab goes out to
look for food for the two of them. The deadly enemy of the
pinna is the cuttlefish. If it can catch the pinna unaware and
with its shell open, the cuttlefish will rush in and devour the
fleshy pinna. So, what is a blind shellfish to do? Fortunately,
the Alphaeus crab is aware of the danger and is quick to act.
At the approach of the cuttlefish, the crab darts back to the
pinna and rushes inside, and the shell is snapped shut, saving
the pinna and his quick-witted Alphaeus crab friend.[23]

[22]Valerian, Homily 3, 4 in *Saint Peter Chrysologus: Selected Sermons and Saint Valerian: Homilies*, vol. 17 of The Fathers of the Church, trans. George E. Ganss, S.J. (New York: Fathers of the Church, 1953), p. 319.

[23]See Simeon Shaw, *Nature Displayed in the Heavens and on the Earth* (London: G. and W.B. Whitaker, 1823), p. 145.

Such an example illustrates well what Pythagoras, the Greek philosopher and mathematician, said about friendship: that it unites "one soul in two bodies". And Saint Thomas Aquinas gave another insightful description of friendship: "A friend is like another self."[24]

So it is not surprising that Saint Augustine complains in his *Confessions* that after he lost a boyhood friend to sickness and death, he felt himself to be only half alive.[25]

Similar Traits

The notion that a friend shares our interests suggests that the friend somehow also resembles us. Aristotle pointed out the importance of similar age and similar education: "Two things that contribute greatly to friendship are a common upbringing and similarity of age."[26] And Confucius thought it important that friends be of the same social status: "The Master said,... 'Have no friends not equal to yourself.' "[27]

But of course there can be other links that we simply may not even recognize when we first meet a friend. When the nineteenth-century British writer and convert to Catholicism Gilbert Keith Chesterton was about fourteen years old, attending Saint Paul's School, he and his classmate Edmund Clerihew Bentley met on the playground and for some reason began punching each other. The next day they again began to fight, and suddenly one of them quoted a line from a poem by Lord Thomas

---

[24] Thomas Aquinas, *Summa Theologica*, I-II, 77, 4, rep. 4.
[25] Augustine, *Confessions*, bk. 4, chaps. 4–6.
[26] Aristotle, *Nicomachean Ethics*, 8, 12.
[27] Confucius, *Analects*, 1, 8.

Macauley. The other quoted the next line. Both were astonished that the other knew the poem. They stopped fighting, and a friendship ensued that lasted over the years. They both had a love for literature and a sense of humor that they enjoyed sharing, and both of them cultivated high ideals.[28] What began in an adversarial context developed into a strong lifelong friendship because of what they had in common.

Augustine talked of the many things that seemed to seal his friendship with others: talking and laughing together; doing each other favors; reading books together; acting silly or talking earnestly together; disagreeing with each other, but in a respectful way "as a person might with his own self"; more often showing agreement with each other; sometimes teaching the other, sometimes learning from him; being impatient till an absent friend would return; welcoming the returning friend with joy. These and other things come from the heart of those who love each other. They can be detected in facial expressions, in speech, in the eyes, in a thousand pleasing gestures[29] and poured out as "so much fuel to melt our souls together, and out of many make but one".[30]

Augustine went on to say that in the beginning he and a certain friend of whom he writes were not all that close, but in time their friendship grew "exceedingly sweet, being heated by the fervor of similar interests". It was after only a year of this closest of friendships that this young man died. Augustine had lost a friendship, as he says, "sweeter to me than all the sweetnesses of this life".[31]

[28] See Alzina Stone Dale, *The Outline of Sanity* (Grand Rapids, Mich.: Eerdmans, 1982), p. 23.

[29] Augustine, *Confessions*, 4, 8, 13.

[30] Ibid., 4, 4, 7.

[31] Ibid.

But promoting mutual interest goes beyond the material and the physical. The values shared must include a
mutual appreciation for the central place of God in human
life and the benefits of sharing faith together.

Perhaps it was the experience of this kind of friendship
that led Augustine to say somewhere in his writings, "One
loving heart sets another on fire."

Saint Teresa of Avila (1515–1582), who was the first
woman declared a Doctor of the Church, reformed the
Carmelite Order in Spain. She saw that finding someone
who shared one's love for Christ could benefit one's prayer
life: "I would counsel those who practice prayer to seek,
at least in the beginning, friendship and association with
other persons having the same interest. This is something
most important even though the association may be only
to help one another with prayers."[32] And she gives the
reason for her advice: "If someone begins to give himself
to God, there are so many to criticize him that he needs to
seek companionship to defend himself until he is so strong
that it is no longer a burden for him to suffer this criticism.
And if he doesn't seek this companionship, he will find
himself in much difficulty."[33]

This same insight led Saint Clement of Alexandria many
centuries earlier to compare a good friend to a pair of earmuffs or to a blindfold:

> [Christ] the Divine Teacher has some suggestions as to
> how to avoid listening to bad things or looking at them.
> He suggests self-restraint for his children who are involved
> in the battle with those kinds of things. He recommends

[32] Teresa of Avila, *The Book of Her Life*, vol. 1 of *The Collected Works of
St. Teresa of Avila*, trans. Kieran Kavanaugh, O.C.D., and Otilio Rodriguez,
O.C.D. (Washington, D.C.: ICS Publications, 1976), p. 64.

[33] Ibid., p. 65.

"earmuffs" so that lewd ideas can't get into the soul and end up hurting it. He also says we should look only at good things, adding that it would be better to blunder with one's feet than with one's eyes.... So what are these "earmuffs"? What are the "blinders" for eyes that tend to wander? Having friendship with good people, and refusing to listen to those who would lead us astray from truth. One poet has said, "Bad company ruins good morals."[34]

A person sharing only the highest spiritual values with his dearest friends would not want, through indecency, to scandalize them or prove himself disloyal to what they all hold dear. Partners in the deepest friendship, then, cherish the same spiritual values: "Whoever fears the Lord directs his friendship aright, for as he is, so is his neighbor also" (Sir 6:17).

Yet we need to avoid excluding others. Christianity would be a rather isolated clique if we associated only with the most morally and spiritually perfect. Can it be that it is sufficient that we understand our own values and where we wish to go with them and with which people we can share them? Knowing those things fortifies us against the relationships that could threaten those values.

My deepest friendships have been with the people who shared my most deeply held values. In my late forties I discovered where a childhood playmate had moved, and I went to visit with him. I found, however, that he and I had almost no values in common. He had no particular appreciation for religion. He was a vocal bigot. He relished plans by which he could cheat other people, particularly

[34]Clement of Alexandria, *Christ the Educator*, 2, 6. Clement lived around A.D. 150 to 215. He founded a school of Christian thought that tried to understand the teachings of Jesus in terms of the philosophy that was being taught in Egypt at the time.

those in government, out of their money. His main goals
in life centered on gaining wealth. It was not long before
our conversation came to a standstill. Two visits with him
were enough to convince me that we did not have enough
in common to resume our childhood friendship.

Yet Jesus did not want his disciples to avoid society in
general. He prayed to his Father, "I do not pray that you
should take them out of the world, but that you should
keep them from the evil one" (Jn 17:15). And Paul cautions against refusing to associate with people who do not
share our faith:

> I wrote to you in my letter not to associate with immoral
> men; not at all meaning the immoral of this world, or the
> greedy and robbers, or idolaters, since then you would
> need to go out of the world. But rather I wrote to you not
> to associate with any one who bears the name of brother
> if he is guilty of immorality or greed, or is an idolater,
> reviler, drunkard, or robber—not even to eat with such a
> one. (1 Cor 5:9–11)

Paul was making the distinction between maneuvering
through society in general and spending too much time
with uncommitted Christians. We know full well that
there are many people in society who do not share our
views or respect our values. With them we must be cau-
tious. But Paul has no kind words for the fellow Christian
who has no values and who might influence us to be just
as lukewarm. Today his approach might be seen as rather
"holier than thou": the uncommitted Christian who does
not know Christ needs as much outreach and invitation as
the non-Christian who does not know Christ.

A Christian has to be an apostle who lives out the gospel
in such a way that all may see it. For that very reason we

cannot disassociate ourselves from people "in the world".
It would be the end of apostolic outreach. Rather, we are
to be "wise as serpents and innocent as doves" (Mt 10:16).

Common Bonds

The goal of friendship is to establish a bond with the friend.
Common experiences, common values, mutual interest,
and mutual respect help establish that communion. But the
more intimate the bond, the deeper the friendship will be.

To have a deep bond with another, we must reveal a
great deal about ourselves. We must be able to share confi-
dences. And to do that, we must be able to trust the other
person not only to respect what we say and to respect
our privacy but also to be understanding and forgiving.

To discover that a friend has betrayed us is the greatest
wound to friendship. Saint Jerome was a great Scripture
scholar who lived at the end of the fourth century and
at the beginning of the fifth. One of the guests at the
hospice that Saint Jerome built in Bethlehem was a ruf-
fian named Sabinianus. While Jerome gave him shelter,
Sabinianus was busy seducing a virgin in the convent
that Jerome had built next door. Sabinianus first seduced
her while he was keeping vigil at the Shrine of the Nativ-
ity, writing her love letters that she would take from him
via a string she let down from her window, and he seduced
her again at the Chapel of the Angel.

Jerome learned about it when the man's love letters
to the girl were discovered. Sabinianus prostrated himself
before Jerome, begged forgiveness, and promised to seclude
himself in the desert and repent, and Jerome forgave him.

Later it was discovered that Sabinianus made a profession out of seduction. He had seduced the wife of a

general, who had discovered it upon his return from a war, and the general himself helped hold the ax that cut off his wife's head. Meanwhile, Sabinianus escaped, as he did from Bethlehem, flaunting himself throughout Syria, as Jerome says, "clothed in fine linen, his fingers laden with rings, his teeth carefully brushed, his thin hair elaborately arranged over his round forehead and his bull neck enclosed in rolls of fat". Jerome remarked that his forgiveness of the man was a mistake and that he should have beaten him to death![35] Saint Jerome probably did not actually mean he would have beaten Sabinianus to death, but his words carried the energy of his anger at being betrayed.

Still a person cannot spend his life distrusting friends. "It is more disgraceful to distrust one's friends than to be deceived by them."[36]

The Roman myth of Psyche explains how mistrust can ruin a relationship. Psyche was the most beautiful of the three daughters of an earthly king. Men were so enthralled with her beauty that they forgot to worship the goddess Venus. This, of course, made Venus angry and jealous. She sent her son, Cupid, the god of love, down to earth to punish Psyche by making her fall in love with some wretched beast. But the moment Cupid saw Psyche, he himself fell in love with her.

While Psyche's two sisters were soon married to kings themselves, no man came forward to marry Psyche. Cupid would use none of his arrows to cause any man to love her, though many admired her. Worried about his daughter,

---

[35] Robert Payne, *The Fathers of the Western Church* (London: Heinemann, 1952), pp. 122–23.

[36] Maxime 84, in François de La Rochefoucauld, *Reflexions ou Sentences et Maximes Morales* (1665).

Psyche's father consulted the oracle of Apollo. There he was given the message that Psyche could marry only a winged creature, that she should be prepared for death, and that she should be taken to the top of a hill, where the winged creature was to find her.

Preparations were made, and Psyche was left to her fate, but kind Zephyr, the gentle west wind, lifted her and set her down in a beautiful meadow in front of a magnificent palace of gold, silver, and jewels. She entered the palace, and, although she saw no one, voices told her to bathe and to dine and entertained her with celestial music. Finally, the voices told her that her new husband would come to her in the night.

She was delighted with her new companion of life, but could not see him in the dark. It was the same way every night. She felt at peace and secure with him but could never see him. He warned her that the moment she could see him, their relationship would be ended.

Psyche had a longing to see her two sisters again. Reluctantly, her invisible husband let her send Zephyr to fetch the women. Their reunion, however, soon turned into an occasion of envy for the two sisters. Although they were married to kings, their wealth was nothing like that of Psyche.

On their next visit, the sisters told Psyche that she was in grave danger. They spoke more from envy than from conviction. They said she had indeed married the winged creature, that that was why she could never be permitted to see him, and that someday the creature would turn on her and devour her. This caused Psyche to feel fear deep in her soul. Her sisters gave her a sharp knife and a lamp. They told her that she must wait until her husband had fallen asleep, then at once shine the lamp on him and kill him with the knife.

Psyche was prepared to do as her sisters suggested. But when she lit the lamp, she saw that her husband was none other than the beautiful god of love himself, Cupid. So bedazzled was she with his beauty that she let some of the oil from her lamp drip onto his shoulder. He awoke with a start, recognized he had been found out, and winged away from Psyche. His words to her were: "Love cannot live where there is lack of trust!"[37]

Saint Aelred says that true friends have the common bond of their love for Christ:

> Let anyone of us who finds it pleasant to enjoy our friends see to it that we enjoy them in the Lord, not in the world or in pleasure of the flesh but in joyfulness of spirit. But, you ask, what does it mean to enjoy "in the Lord"? About the Lord, the apostle Paul said: "By God he has been made for us wisdom, sanctification and justice." Since the Lord is wisdom, sanctification and justice, to find enjoyment in the Lord is to find enjoyment in wisdom, sanctification and justice.[38]

In other words, friends are to share the same Christian values, making friendship with Christ the highest good they share.

Sacrifice

Just as I have wanted to give my friends gifts to express my regard and affection for them, I welcome opportunities to make sacrifices for them. A sacrifice is a "more expensive" gift. Jesus said, "Greater love has no man than this, that a man lay down his life for his friends" (Jn 15:13).

[37] See Edith Hamilton, *Mythology* (Boston: Little, Brown, 1969), pp. 92–96.
[38] Aelred of Rievaulx, *Mirror of Charity*, p. 42.

A doctor who had taken his family to a restaurant was accosted on the sidewalk after the meal. Two robbers took his daughter's purse and then demanded that his wife come with them. The doctor threw his arms around his wife, a shot was fired, and the robbers fled. A taxi was not available, so the family began walking. Three blocks later the doctor collapsed from a gunshot wound in his side. He had said nothing about it. But his action to protect his wife and daughter said volumes about his dedication to them.

Sometimes when it appears that I have been the one making the sacrifice to maintain a friendly relationship with someone else, I discover that my friend has made plenty of sacrifice for me. An old Mexican fable tells of a woman who had very misshapen hands. Because of this, her son felt ashamed before other boys when his mother was around. He even went so far as to ask her to stay away from his friends. Shortly thereafter, his father told him a story: "Once there was a beautiful young mother with a small baby whom she loved with all her heart. One night a fire broke out in their home, and the young lady rushed to the room of her infant son. Already flames were breaking out around the crib. The mother began slapping them out with her bare hands to save her son. And that son," emphasized the father, "is you." After that, the son had a new appreciation for his mother's beauty and said she had the prettiest hands in the world.

Saint John of the Cross (1542–1591), a Doctor of the Church and the spiritual director of Saint Teresa of Avila, said, "For he who truly loves is satisfied then when his whole self, all he is, all he can be, all he has, and all he can acquire, is spent in the service of his love; and the greater that service, the greater is his pleasure in giving it."[39]

---

[39]John of the Cross, *The Living Flame of Love*, 3, 2.

49

Loyalty to the Friend

Communion with a friend must be not only deep but also enduring. Loyalty to the friend is an essential element of authentic friendship. I have, at least internally, made pledges of loyalty to my very best friends. The pledge goes something like this: "I will be your friend no matter what you do or don't do, no matter how I feel or don't feel." We have a natural tendency to feel affection for someone as long as he does what fits into our "program" for him. How many times have we been given the silent treatment because we did not do something someone wanted us to do or because we did something at which he took offense? True friendship stands apart from feelings. It is a commitment. In that sense, it is an act of faith.

I once heard a story about two brothers who served on the front during the First World War. One was critically wounded in battle. His brother asked the sergeant permission to retrieve him.

"He is probably already dead," said the sergeant. "Don't risk your life to look for him."

The soldier could not restrain himself. He went ahead, located his brother, and dragged him back to camp, already dead. The sergeant felt satisfied that he had given good advice.

"You see," he said to the young soldier, "I told you your brother was dead. What good did it do to risk your life like that?"

"When I reached my brother," the faithful young man said, "he was still alive. He saw me and said, 'I knew you would come for me.' So, although I did not save my brother from dying, I saved his faith in me."

The Wisdom books of the Old Testament offer us plenty of advice about loyalty to friends:

A friend loves at all times, and a brother is born for
  adversity. (Prov 17:17)
There are friends who pretend to be friends, but there
  is a friend who sticks closer than a brother. (Prov
  18:24)
Forsake not an old friend, for a new one does not compare with him. (Sir 9:10)

In his autobiography, *The Seven Storey Mountain*, Thomas
Merton talked about how he and his friends, when they
were about ten years old, would try to keep Thomas' little
brother, John Paul, and his little brother's friends, all about
five years old, far away from them. They did not want to
associate with "the little kids". When the little boy tried
to follow him, Thomas and his friends threw rocks at him.
Little John Paul stood there crying and bewildered. He
only wanted to be with his brother, and he did not know
why Thomas had rejected him.[40]

Merton used the incident to meditate on the value of
disinterested love, which goes beyond how we feel about a
person and enables us to love him unconditionally, simply
for who he is. The incident reminded Merton of sin, our
rejecting disinterested love simply because we do not want
it, and he surmised that perhaps we do this because disinterested love reminds us that we all need love, and we do
not want to admit that. It is too humiliating to say we need
someone's love.

Patience

To remain loyal to a friend sometimes requires extraordinary patience. We must learn to put up with the

[40]See Thomas Merton, *The Seven Storey Mountain* (San Diego: Harcourt,
Brace, Jovanovich, 1976), p. 23.

imperfections of others. An Italian proverb observes, "He who will have none but a perfect brother must resign himself to remain brotherless." Or as the Sacred Scriptures tell us, "Better is a dinner of herbs where love is than a fatted ox and hatred with it" (Prov 15:17).

Friendship makes all inconveniences bearable. Aquinas said, "Whatever we do or suffer for a friend is pleasant, because love is the principle cause of pleasure."[41]

Joseph Cardinal Bernardin, archbishop of Chicago in the last part of the twentieth century, learned the lesson of patience in love from his father:

> One memory in particular that I want to share happened when I was four or five. It was summertime, and our family was visiting friends. My father had recently undergone cancer-related surgery on his left shoulder, and he was wearing a bandage under a white short-sleeved shirt. I was sitting on a metal railing on the porch of our friends' home, when suddenly I fell backwards, hit the ground, and started crying. My father immediately jumped over the rail and picked me up. As he held me in his arms, I could see blood soaking through his shirt. He paid no attention to himself; all he wanted was to be sure I was all right.[42]

Here we see the meaning of patience: willingness to put up with suffering; in this case, a father's willingness to suffer for the sake of his son.

Saint Thomas Aquinas offered this insight: "What we do from love we do most willingly."[43] And Saint Bernard of Clairvaux said, "Nothing is impossible to those who believe (Mt 17:20). Nothing is difficult for those who love."[44]

---

[41] Thomas Aquinas, *Summa Theologica*, I-II, 32, 6.
[42] Joseph Cardinal Bernardin, *The Gift of Peace* (New York: Image Books, 1998), p. 62.
[43] Thomas Aquinas, *Summa Theologica*, I-II, 114, 4.
[44] Bernard of Clairvaux, *On Conversion*, 21, 38.

Forgiveness

All our earthly friends are human and capable of error, just as we are. If we want to be able to retain those friends, we have to learn to apologize and to forgive.

Jesus has set the standard for our forgiveness: "Then Peter came up and said to him, 'Lord, how often shall my brother sin against me, and I forgive him? As many as seven times?' Jesus said to him, 'I do not say to you seven times, but seventy-seven times'" (cf. Mt 18:21–22). Jesus did not literally mean seventy-seven times, of course. Seven was considered the perfect number, and seventy-seven meant multiples of that. Jesus could have said, "Forgive any number of times. Never stop forgiving."

It is especially in Jesus' teaching on forgiving others that Christianity sets itself apart. The natural human tendency is to take revenge on those who have offended us. Jesus teaches that we must break the cycle of violence and hatred by injecting forgiveness.

Another tendency that calls for understanding and forgiveness in friendship is jealousy. Jealousy is part of our animal nature. Across the alley from a house where I once lived, there was a lady with three dogs. The big black dog was the dominant one. The other two, a gray German shepherd and a tan terrier, were made to feel the black dog's dominance. Whenever we took our trash to the dumpster in the alley, the three dogs went mad with joy to see us and leapt about and barked, hoping to attract our attention. But when I would go over to pet them, the big black dog wanted all the petting. If I attempted to pet one of the other dogs, he snarled and snapped at them, and they cowered and slunk away in clear dejection.

When I have felt a particular fondness for someone, I have also felt a tinge of jealousy when others have shown a fondness for or closeness to him. Intellectually I understand that I should not act on that feeling, but it is an automatic feeling, all part of that mechanism within us that leads, for some people, to the exclusive relationship of marriage. We see this tendency in children's desire to be preferred over their siblings by their parents.

To return to the notion of forgiveness, there is nothing that I would not forgive my friend, because I value his friendship and never want to lose it. Similarly, Jesus teaches us that we are all to be friends of one another, no matter what the circumstances. I remember seeing a story on TV about a woman who gave cookies to hikers who came through her property, which adjoined a bicycle trail. She told the reporter who interviewed her, "Strangers are only friends you haven't met yet."

Can you imagine what would happen if Israelis and Arabs decided they are friends who have to work things out? Or if this became the mind-set of the people in the Balkans, or of the Pakistanis and the Indians? Or the people of various races and ethnic groups in any country, including the United States? What if they simply regarded each other as friends who have not gotten to know each other well enough yet?

I hope that God will give me the humility to initiate the process of reconciliation even if I do not think a conflict is my fault.

Seeing to the Best Interests of the Friend

Fraternal Correction

Sometimes love must raise a warning: "He who has an ear, let him hear what the Spirit says to the churches" (Rev 2:29; 3:6, 13, 22), the angel says in the book of Revelation, and then lays it on the line how the members of the representative churches around Asia Minor at the end of the first century were failing to live up to their faith.

It would be a mistake to imagine that loving our friends means that we can never criticize what they have done or that their criticism of us is disloyal. The Jewish Midrash (a commentary on the Hebrew Scriptures) assures us, "Love without criticism is not love."

Saint Aelred said some people "take enjoyment in flattery, patting each other on the back and conniving with each other. While taking care not to offend one another, they incur each other's ruin, because they do not enjoy themselves in the liberty of justice or in the Lord."[45] This "liberty of justice" means truth. Exaggerated flattery is misleading, and wanting to please another or simply not to displease him so as to remain in his good graces, no matter what happens to him as a consequence of his actions, is not truthful or just. It is not a relationship lived "in the Lord".

Jesus lays down the rules of how we are to correct others:

> If your brother sins against you, go and tell him his fault, between you and him alone. If he listens to you, you have gained your brother. But if he does not listen, take one or two others along with you, that every word may be confirmed by the evidence of two or three witnesses. If he refuses to listen to them, tell it to the Church; and if he refuses to listen even to the Church, let him be to you as a Gentile and a tax collector. (Mt 18:15–17)

Nevertheless, we must be careful that our correction of others does not become self-righteous and overbearing. Saint Francis de Sales wrote:

[45] Aelred of Rievaulx, *Mirror of Charity*, p. 43.

At the beginning of his career Saint Bernard[46] was full of
rigor and sharpness toward those put under his direction
and would tell them they must leave the body behind and
come to him in soul only. When he heard their confessions he reprimanded with extraordinary severity faults
of every kind, no matter how slight, and urged on those
poor apprentices to perfection in such a way that instead
of pushing them on he pulled them back. They lost heart
and breath at seeing themselves unrelentingly driven up
so steep and high an ascent. Philothea, note that it was
most ardent zeal for perfect purity that induced this great
saint to adopt this method. His zeal was a great virtue but
a virtue open to criticism. Hence God himself in a holy
vision corrected him and infused into his soul a spirit so
meek, gentle, amiable, and tender that he was completely
changed by it. He not only charged himself with being too
strict and severe but became so gracious and considerate
to everyone that he became "all things to all men" in
order to save all of them.[47]

I hesitate to correct others, perhaps to some degree out
of cowardice, but more so because if it is done over too
slight a cause or too frequently, people classify me as a
nag and simply will not pay any attention to me. Unless a
person has asked for advice on his own initiative, fraternal
correction should be reserved for situations in which the
person's eternal salvation is at stake.

Father Bernard Häring, a Redemptorist moral theologian, was always criticizing members of the Curia of the
Vatican (the administrative center of the Church) for being,
in his estimation, less than Christian. He was once asked
if he ever voiced his criticisms directly to Curia members
instead of about them. He replied that about once a year

---

[46] Cf. William of Saint Thierry, *Vita et tres gestae sancti Bernardi*, 1, 4, 6.
[47] Francis de Sales, *Introduction to the Devout Life*, 3, 2.

he would go to the Congregation for the Faith and tell them that he disputed some teaching they had published during the year. He said that he did this so seldom because otherwise he would gain the reputation of a nag and no one would pay any attention to him. I think his published criticisms earned him that reputation anyway, and they still did not listen to him.

I look on fraternal correction as the jokers in a deck of cards. Jokers are wild cards that you play at strategically important times, and you can play only two of them, compared with the four of each of the other cards in the deck. Until the time comes to play the joker, you go along with the game.

That leads to a fair amount of dysfunction in a community, but it is probably all that can be hoped for realistically. We just have to learn to tolerate a lot. We have to remind ourselves that other people are our brothers and sisters, our friends, and tolerate their faults—except, however, in cases of serious moral threat.

Some years back we Redemptorists in what was then the Midwest province of the United States introduced a drive to aid our members who were suffering from alcoholism. It required community intervention, and for the most part it worked. There is a procedure we follow in giving these interventions. All the members of the community begin documenting the times when a confrere is drunk. They line up a treatment program for him. They keep the provincial superiors advised. And then, on a particular occasion, when the colleague in question has fallen again, they all confront him together. He has no choice but to go along with the treatment. After many years of using this approach, there is very little evidence of that sort of problem among the Redemptorists of our province today, thank God. But at one time the problem was too common.

If I were in a community in which a priest or religious brother were engaged in any sort of immoral behavior, and especially if it could cause scandal, I would feel obligated to do something about it. And if I were the culprit, I would hope that others would intervene to help save me. But, in general, grave moral situations are not the order of the day in our communities.

Sometimes friendship itself eliminates the need to correct a friend. I have noticed that if close friends even thought I did not like something they were doing, they would try to change what they were doing without my saying anything to them. One young man in our postulant community admired me and cherished my favorable opinion of him. He noticed one day that I was not happy with some little thing he had done, and, even though I had said nothing to him about it, he corrected it immediately. Of course, it is still good to discuss the situation, but the regard that friendship creates makes it easier to do so.

That would be the ideal situation in our communities and families. If we truly loved one another and were friends, we would give each other permission to speak up when we saw something amiss. The fact that we cannot do so shows that our friendships are still in need of a great deal of maturing.

Doing What Is Best for the Friend

We do not always want what is best for ourselves. A good friend will not give us something harmful but will insist on our having what would be helpful to us.

Many times I have said no to beggars who ask me for money but who are clearly inebriated. I was visiting one of our communities one day, going in the back door with

a bag of potato chips in my hand. I was stopped by a very
drunk fellow who wanted to ask not what time it was but
what day it was! At any rate, the real purpose of his detain-
ing me was to say that he had no food in his house and he
needed money. I pointed out that I was a visitor and had
no access to the food bank, but that he could have the rest
of my potato chips. He said he really did not want that,
but that he wanted the money and could not understand
(here he was letting flow some rather large tears) how the
Church could let down a faithful Catholic. I gave him
the chips anyway, went inside, and closed the door firmly.
He staggered away.

In his mind, the man saw it as in his best interest to ask
for money (soon to be converted into more alcohol). I
knew it was in his best interest not to be given the means
to continue drinking.

Saint Clement of Alexandria had an interesting
observation:

> Those who are very affable in their relations with others
> really show less love simply because they never become
> provoked, while those who administer rebuke for the
> good of someone else, although they are disagreeable at
> the moment, render a service that affects the life after the
> grave. So, too, the Lord is interested, not in promoting
> our present pleasure, but the happiness that is to come.[48]

---

[48] Clement of Alexandria, *Christ the Educator*, 1, 9.

3

FRIENDSHIP WITH OURSELVES

"So whatever you wish that men would do to you, do so to them; for this is the law and the prophets" (Mt 7:12). What is it that we want others to do for us? If we had no notion of what is good for us, we could have no notion of what would be good for others.

It is not a vice to love ourselves. "The origin of friendly relations with others lies in our relations to ourselves", observed the philosopher Aristotle.[1] Saint Thomas Aquinas, following his lead, wrote: "The love with which a person loves himself is the form and root of friendship. For if we have friendship with others it is because we do unto them as we do unto ourselves."[2]

If we did not allow ourselves to acknowledge our hurts and disappointments, we would not understand others when they come to us for consolation in their hurts and disappointments. Saint Bernard of Clairvaux said:

> Those who do not share the troubles of others but, on the contrary, spurn those who weep or mock those who are happy, and do not feel in themselves the feelings of others because they are not moved by their emotion, how

[1] Aristotle, *Ethics*, 9, 4, 8.
[2] Thomas Aquinas, *Summa Theologica*, II-II, 25, 4.

can they find the truth in their neighbors? That common proverb fits them well, "The healthy man does not know what the sick man feels."[3] The man who is well fed does not know what the hungry man feels. The sick man more readily feels with the sick and the hungry man with the hungry. For just as pure truth is seen only with a pure heart, so he who is wretched at heart feels more truly with the wretchedness of his brother.

But to have a heart which is sad because of someone else's wretchedness you must first recognize your neighbor's mind in your own and understand from your own experience how you can help him.[4]

It would be psychologically impossible to love anyone else without properly loving ourselves.

Psychiatrist Carl Jung somewhere said, "My pilgrim's progress during the course of my life has led me down ten thousand ladders until I could reach out the hand of friendship to the little clod of earth that is myself."[5] The first step to holiness, if we understand holiness to mean loving God and other people, is to learn gradually to love ourselves: to seek for and find something about ourselves worth loving.

Priest-psychologist Father Ignace Lepp wrote: "Love for another which included no love of self would not be human; in fact, it is psychologically impossible."[6]

And Dr. M. Scott Peck tells about a study that was done when he was a psychiatrist with the army. Twelve people in their late thirties and early forties from all branches of the service were chosen as subjects of the study. They all

---

[3] Terence, *Andria*, ed. J. Zargeaunt (London, 1953), 309.

[4] Bernard of Clairvaux, *On the Steps of Humility and Pride*, 3, 6.

[5] Ann Casement, *Carl Gustave Jung* (London: Sage Publications, 2001), p. 22.

[6] Ignace Lepp, *Death and Its Mysteries* (New York: Macmillan, 1968), p. 44.

had been unusually successful and still were popular with fellow service members. The army wanted to know the reason for their success. Each was asked to write down, without consulting the others, the three most important things in his life. All twelve wrote "myself" first.[7]

It may be shocking to hear that successful people put themselves first. Jesus has made it clear that the last shall be first and the first last (see Mt 20:16). But there is a real sense in which we must be conscious of who we are; to be able to love God and others as we should, we must come to know ourselves first.

Faith in the Friend

First of all, we must prize being loved.

John Knowles' 1959 novel, *A Separate Peace*, is about two sixteen-year-old boys who attend summer courses at a boys' school in New England. They are roommates. Finny has a magnetic personality, so he goes around, as the author says, with a group the size of a hockey team about him. He charms students and professors alike.

He has charmed his roommate, Gene. When Finny jumps out of the branches of a tall tree into a river, he challenges his four companions to do the same. Only Gene responds, as if hypnotized, almost against his will. But his going along with Finny seals him and Finny as friends.

But not forever. There is an underlying resentment in Gene against the control that Finny is able to exercise over him. When Finny successfully entices him to neglect his

[7]M. Scott Peck, M.D., *Further Along the Road Less Traveled* (New York: Simon and Schuster, 1993), p. 88.

studies to the point of flunking an important exam and losing academic status in his class, Gene begins to wonder about Finny's motivation. He comes to believe that Finny does not love him as a friend at all, that Finny simply does not want anyone to be superior to him, including in academics.

Gene's resentment of Finny comes to a head when they are back in the tree and Finny is about to take the leap once again. Instinctively, Gene jounces the tree branch, knocking Finny to the ground below. Finny, to this point a superb natural athlete, suffers a shattered leg that will exclude him from sports for the rest of his life.

Gene comes to discover that Finny does not flag in his friendship for Gene. Finny always, genuinely, simply wanted to be Gene's friend. But it was Gene's loss of faith in Finny that caused him to forfeit a most precious friendship and an important part of his life.

At its base, faith is accepting the love of a friend. It means setting aside our doubts and wariness. It means making a commitment to regard the other as a friend. Saint Augustine said that real, loyal faith in the love of a friend accepts that love even before it has been tested by trial. And even when that loyalty and friendship are proven in the friend during trial, it is still an act of faith on our part.[8] Only when we are able to accept love with faith can we progress toward love of neighbor or of God.

Psychologist Erich Fromm has speculated that a reason people might not accept love from others is that they would then have to return love. "While one is consciously afraid of not being loved, the real, though usually unconscious, fear is that of loving."[9]

---

[8] Augustine, *On Faith in Things Unseen*, 3.
[9] Erich Fromm, *The Art of Loving* (New York: Harper, 1956), p. 127.

Some ancient Roman writers were wary of gifts offered by others. One of them, Martial, a poet who lived about the time of the apostles, said, "Gifts are like hooks."[10] And another writer of the time, Publilius Syrus, commented: "To ask a favor is to sell one's freedom."[11]

A story in the Talmud, the primary Jewish commentary on the Hebrew Scriptures, tells of a rabbi who was habitually humiliated by a nagging wife. The rabbi finally took a friend's advice and divorced her. Almost immediately she took up with a policeman who promised to support and love her. But before long, the officer became blind and impoverished. The couple now had no choice but for the officer to use his blindness as an excuse for begging. Many times it failed to add to their coffers.

On one occasion the nag led her blind husband up and down every street and alley in the town, with the exception of one, and they received nothing for all their best begging efforts.

"Is there no other street on which we may beg?" asked the almost desperate blind man.

"There is one," the woman answered, "but I don't want to go there, because it is the street on which my ex-husband lives."

The policeman insisted that they go down that street as well.

The rabbi, the ex-husband of the woman, saw them and aided them. He gave them a house to live in and provided them with food for the rest of their lives. Nevertheless the woman felt so ashamed of being supported by her ex-husband that she lamented, "Was it not better to

---

[10] Martial, *Epigrams*, 5, 18, 7.

[11] Publilius Syrus in Charles Noel Douglas, *Forty Thousand Quotations, Prose, and Poetical* (London: George G. Harrap and Co., 1904), p. 718.

suffer the pain of my external condition than the pain in my inner self?"[12]

Despite our reluctance to receive help from others, sometimes we simply need it. And it benefits both parties mutually by creating a bond that otherwise would not have been there. Saint Clement of Rome goes so far as to say that society itself works better for the mixing of social classes when one group helps the other: "Important people cannot exist without less important people. All get mixed together, for the benefit of all."[13]

I do not want to stray too far from the main point, however: we need to acknowledge our need for each other and the gift of love that we receive from others. To accept the love of another is an act of faith.

Our Dignity Comes from God's Love

The absolute truth about ourselves is that we are lovable because God loves us. God, who is truth itself, declares that we are lovable. And not even we ourselves can deny that truth. In a very real sense all our value comes from God's having created and redeemed us.

Once a farmer was choosing hired hands to go with him to the field. He had already chosen six men and called a seventh to join him from a large crowd of unemployed standing in the village plaza, waiting to be hired. This seventh man, who wanted work very badly, became quite proud to believe he had been chosen over the others. He put the question to the farmer: "Did you choose me

---

[12] "The Tractate Ketubot," Yerushalmi 11:3 [34b], in *The Talmud: Selected Writings*, trans. Ben Zion Bokser (New York: Paulist Press, 1989), pp. 150–51.

[13] Clement of Rome, *Letter to the Corinthians*, 37, 4.

because I work harder than the others or because of my superior intelligence?"

The farmer answered, "I chose you because you are the only one small enough to fit in the wagon with the other six big men."

We might be chagrined to find out why God chose to give us the gift of human life over other possible men he could have created, but God created us because he already loved us before we came into being.

Saint Thomas Aquinas is said to have observed: "Just as a heavy weight cannot naturally rise of itself, unless moved by another, so the human heart which by nature tends to inferior things, cannot of itself lift itself to heavenly things, unless it is moved by God the Father."[14]

For whatever reason, God considers us lovable. God has lifted us above our nothingness and given us existence. The fact that he has done so is part of the mystery of love.

Humility Is Truth

Humility is a virtue valued widely not only by Christians and Jews but by all societies. To love ourselves might seem the opposite of humility. But Aquinas, from his own thought and from contemplating the writings of another great saint, has given the proper finesse to the question of humility: "Well ordered self-love, by which man desires a fitting good for himself, is right and natural; but it is inordinate self-love, leading to the contempt of God, that Augustine puts as the cause of sin."[15] There is such a thing

---

[14] Thomas Aquinas, quoted in E. C. McEniry, O.P., *Meditations of St. Thomas Aquinas, O.P.* (Columbus, Ohio: Long's College, 1951), p. 229.

[15] Thomas Aquinas, *Summa Theologica*, I-II, 77, 4, rep.1.

as valid "love for self". Without that attitude, self-hatred
or even indifference toward what is really good for us
would destroy us.

Saint Bernard of Clairvaux also saw humility as fundamental and called it "the food of the spiritual life": "The
first food, then, is humility. It purges by its bitterness.
The second is the food of love, which consoles by its
sweetness. The third is the food of contemplation, solid
and strengthening."[16]

In her autobiography, Saint Teresa of Avila has very
similar advice:

> Along [the] path of prayer, self-knowledge and the thought
> of one's sins is the bread with which all palates must be fed
> no matter how delicate they may be; they cannot be sus-
> tained without this bread. It must be eaten within bounds,
> nonetheless. Once a soul sees that it is now submissive and
> understands clearly that it has nothing good of itself and is
> aware both of being ashamed before so great a King and of
> repaying so little of the great amount it owes him—what
> need is there to waste time here? We must go on to other
> things that the Lord places before us; and there is no rea-
> son to leave them aside, for his Majesty knows better than
> we what is fitting for us to eat.[17]

Saint Teresa is saying that it is true that we are incapable
of doing anything worthwhile on our own and that in fact
we fail miserably many times, but once we realize this, we
should not stop there. The other part of the reality is that
our strength lies in God's grace and love working in us,
and these can make us unimaginably fruitful.

Humility is best described as accepting the full truth about
ourselves, the good and the bad. Thus, to have humility,

---

[16]Bernard of Clairvaux, *On the Steps of Humility and Pride*, 2, 5.
[17]Teresa of Avila, *The Book of Her Life*, 13, 15.

we must have a love of the truth. Saint Paul laments the attitude of those who "are to perish, because they refused to love the truth and so be saved" (2 Thess 2:10).

I have detected in my most beloved friends a real humility in that they have a good sense of humor about themselves, yet they also have a sense of their own value. A person who can laugh at his foibles but understand himself as lovable in God's sight is a humble person.

God's Love for Us

The most important fact about ourselves is that God has loved us from all eternity. It was his love for the idea of us that caused him to create each of us in the first place. "From eternity", said Pope John Paul II, "God has thought of us and has loved us as unique individuals."[18]

I would like to dwell for a few minutes on some of the ways God has shown that extraordinary love toward us. Saint Alphonsus observed:

> He went so far as to become an infant, to become poor, even so far as openly to die the death of a malefactor upon the cross. He went yet farther, even to hide himself under the appearance of bread, in order to become our constant companion and unite himself intimately to us: "He who eats my flesh and drinks my blood abides in me, and I in him" (Jn 6:56). In a word, he loves you as much as though he had no love but toward yourself alone.[19]

---

[18] John Paul II, *Of the Lay Faithful in the Church and in the World* (*Christifideles Laici*), 58.

[19] Alphonsus de Liguori, *The Way to Converse Always and Familiarly with God*, in *The Way of Salvation and Perfection*, vol. 2 of *The Complete Works of Saint Alphonsus de Liguori*, ed. Rev. Eugene Grimm, C.Ss.R. (Brooklyn, N.Y.: Redemptorist Fathers, 1926), p. 392. I have substituted the contemporary English RSV-CE2 translation of Bible passages for those that Fr. Grimm used in his translation of Saint Alphonsus' works.

The experience of God's love in his gift of creation

Consider these facts that illustrate the grandeur of the vast universe:

- Some of the light we see in space left its source 1.5 million years ago.
- The universe may be 12 to 15 billion years old.
- There are more than 100 thousand million known galaxies.
- Some galaxies move away from the earth at 15,000 miles per second; some stars approach the earth at 12 miles per second.
- One light-year, the distance light can travel in a year, is 6 trillion miles.
- The Milky Way is at least 600,000 light-years, or 3,600 million billion miles, wide.
- There are at least 100 billion stars in the Milky Way.
- The distance between the sun and Pluto is 4 billion miles; at a speed of 6,000 miles per hour, it would take 67 years to travel the distance.
- The most distant galaxy is 10 billion light-years from Earth.
- Earth is 4.5 billion years old.

At the other end of the scale of God's creation, the precision with which God has made the tiniest parts of the tiniest elements is fascinating. Six quarks make up the protons and neutrons of an atom. While the sixth quark is thirty-five times heavier than the fifth quark, it is smaller than a trillionth of the thickness of a human hair and exists for only a trillionth of a trillionth of a second.

Saint Athanasius was patriarch of Alexandria, Egypt, and a Doctor of the Church in the fourth century. He did not have the benefit of such scientific refinement, but he appreciated the beauty of God's creation:

Think of a musician tuning his lyre. By his skill he adjusts high notes to low and intermediate notes to the rest, and produces a series of harmonies. So too the wisdom of God holds the world like a lyre and joins things in the air to those on earth, and things in heaven to those in the air, and brings each part into harmony with the whole.[20]

Saint Thérèse of Lisieux also marveled at the greatness of the Creator by contemplating his creation: "When I was six or seven years old I saw the sea for the first time. This spectacle caused a profound impression on me; I could not take my eyes away from it. Its majesty, the roaring of its waves, all spoke to my soul of the greatness and power of God."[21]

And Saint Augustine is said to have written: "If the work of his hands be so lovely, how much more beautiful must be he who made them."

To some who might object that we see in creation not only the beautiful but the brutal and the violent as well, Saint Augustine responds:

> The goodness of God ... has not been recognized by some ... because there are ... many things, such as fire, frost, wild beasts and so forth, which do not suit but injure this thin-blooded and frail mortality of our flesh.... They do not consider how admirable these things are in their own places, how excellent in their own natures, how beautifully adjusted to the rest of creation, and how much grace they contribute to the universe.... [They do not consider] how serviceable they are even to ourselves, if we use them with a knowledge of their fit adaptations—so that even poisons, which are destructive when used injudiciously,

[20] Athanasius, *A Discourse against the Pagans*, 42.

[21] Thérèse of Lisieux, quoted in Rev. Mauricio Rufino, *A Vademecum of Stories* (New York: Joseph F. Wagner, 1967), p. 6.

become wholesome and medicinal when used in conformity with their qualities and design.[22]

And French thinker Blaise Pascal, who lived in the seventeenth century, said somewhere in his writings: "Nature has some perfections, to show [us] that she is the image of God; and some defects, to show [us] that she is only his image."[23]

But the point of all of this is to recognize that God made all of this *for us*: "Has not everything that you see been made for you?" asked Saint Peter Chrysologus.[24]

And recognizing God's love for us in his creation, we can respond with Saint Augustine: "[Lord,] heaven and earth and all things tell me to love you."[25]

The Incarnation: proof of God's love for us

Pope Paul VI said in his letter on evangelization: "For man the Creator is not an anonymous and remote power; he is the Father: '... that we should be called children of God; and so we are' (1 Jn 3:1; cf. Rom 8:14–17). And thus we are one another's brothers and sisters in God."[26] God has not created the universe and then set it aside, as a watchmaker might wind up a clock and set it on a shelf. God remains intimately involved with his creation and has supreme interest in the life of each of us.

God has proven his love for us by sending Jesus: "In this the love of God was made manifest among us, that God sent his only-begotten Son into the world, so that we

---

[22] Augustine, *City of God*, 11, 22.

[23] Pascal, *Pensees*, vii, in *The Fundamentals of Christian Religion*, trans. W. F. Trotter (New York: E. P. Dutton, 1958), no. 580.

[24] Peter Chrysologus, Sermon 148.

[25] Augustine, *Confessions*, 10, 6.

[26] Paul VI, *On Evangelization in the Modern World (Evangelii Nuntiandi)*, 26.

might live through him" (1 Jn 4:9). And there is that well-known verse of John's Gospel that sums up all of Christian teaching: "For God so loved the world that he gave his only-begotten Son, that whoever believes in him should not perish but have eternal life" (Jn 3:16).

Saint Alphonsus noted: "Before the Incarnation of the Word, man might have doubted whether God loved him with a true love; but after the coming of the Son of God, and after his dying for the love of men, how can we possibly doubt of his love?"[27]

As Saint John Chrysostom said, "God became man simply out of love and mercy for us: the Incarnation had no other motive."[28]

The sacrifice of Jesus: proof of God's love for us

Paul reminded us that Christ's sacrifice is the greatest proof of God's love for us: "But God shows his love for us in that while we were yet sinners Christ died for us" (Rom 5:8). "And walk in love, as Christ loved us and gave himself up for us, a fragrant offering and sacrifice to God" (Eph 5:2). John tells us, "By this we know love, that he laid down his life for us; and we ought to lay down our lives for the brethren" (1 Jn 3:16). According to Paul, in this supreme act of kindness, God's generosity has been revealed: "[B]ut when the goodness and loving kindness of God our Savior appeared, he saved us, not because of deeds done by us in righteousness, but in virtue of his own mercy, by the washing of regeneration and renewal in the Holy Spirit" (Tit 3:4–5).

---

[27] Alphonsus de Liguori, *The Practice of the Love of Jesus Christ*, in *The Holy Eucharist*, vol. 6 of *The Complete Works of Saint Alphonsus de Liguori: The Ascetical Works*, ed. Rev. Eugene Grimm, C.Ss.R. (New York: Benziger Brothers, 1887), p. 299.

[28] John Chrysostom, *On Hebrews*, 5, 1.

Seeing the crucifix so often and hearing about Jesus' sufferings have dulled our appreciation for the actual suffering that Jesus underwent. I would like to refer extensively to a book that reporter Jim Bishop wrote describing the sufferings of Jesus from a medical point of view:

The physician Luke tells us that in the Garden of Olives, "being in an agony [Jesus] prayed more earnestly; and his sweat became like great drops of blood falling down upon the ground" (Lk 22:44). A phenomenon called hematidrosis occurs when a person is in deep fear. Ordinarily, the person loses consciousness during the onset of the condition. If he does not lose consciousness, the subcutaneous capillaries dilate broadly. When they come into contact with the sweat glands, the capillaries burst and it appears that the individual is sweating blood. Usually the blood is exuded from the entire body.[29]

"And they led Jesus to the high priest; and all the chief priests and the elders and the scribes were assembled" (Mk 14:53). This convocation was the Sanhedrin, the governing body of the Jewish people at the time. A prisoner brought before the Great Sanhedrin of the Jewish state would be tied up with rope, his feet tied close enough together to permit a hobbled walk, but not a run. The prisoner would have to stand throughout the entire ordeal.[30]

Once a prisoner was condemned to die, he was subject to being the sport of his captors, since there would be no one to complain to about the rough treatment he might receive in his captivity. The guards were at liberty to slap their prisoner and would take turns at doing so. They might punch him heavily in the chest or stomach, and when he would bend over in pain, hit him in the face. They would also spit at him.[31]

[29]Jim Bishop, *The Day Christ Died* (New York: Harper, 1957), p. 211.
[30]Ibid., p. 227.
[31]Ibid., p. 232.

"Then Pilate took Jesus and scourged him" (Jn 19:1). Generally Roman scourging was administered in place of another punishment. It would stop just short of killing the prisoner and so was called the "halfway death". The prisoner was completely stripped of his clothing and bent double over a thick stone pillar about three feet high. His wrists were tied to two iron rings embedded in the pillar. The whip was a short circular piece of wood with several leather straps attached to it. On the end of each strap a small chunk of bone or a piece of iron chain was sewn. There were no restrictions on which parts of the body could be scourged or on the number of lashes.[32] The body of the prisoner would often be washed with cold water after scourging, not out of compassion, but to revive the prisoner to consciousness.[33]

"And the soldiers plaited a crown of thorns, and put it on his head, and clothed him in a purple robe; they came up to him, saying, 'Hail, King of the Jews!' and struck him with their hands" (Jn 19:2–3). Dried thorns were always kept in pails around the courtyard to be used for starting fires. The Roman soldiers wove a helmet of these thorns that fitted like a skullcap on Jesus' head. Jesus was very likely in a state of shock by this point.[34]

In preparation for crucifixion, a prisoner was stripped naked, except for a loincloth, to increase his humiliation. This also allowed insects to bite and infest his wounded skin as he hung exposed and helpless on the cross.[35]

"Then he handed him over to them to be crucified. So they took Jesus, and he went out, bearing his own cross, to the place called a place of the skull, which is called in Hebrew Golgotha" (Jn 19:16–17). The cross consisted

32 Ibid., p. 291.
33 Ibid., p. 292.
34 Ibid., p. 293.
35 Ibid., p. 308.

of two beams. The crossbeam, called the *patibulum*, was carried by the condemned criminal to the site of execution. The other, about six feet high, called the *stipes crucis*, remained permanently fixed in the ground. The wrists of the criminal were first nailed to the crossbeam, which was then hoisted atop the upright beam to form a T.[36] The nails were five inches long. The prisoner was thrust backward by guards, his neck pressed against the crossbeam, and the soldiers kneeled on the insides of his elbows as they hammered the nails.[37] In Jesus' case, as he fell, the crown of thorns tore into his scalp.[38] The criminal's legs were buckled and his feet nailed to the upright beam,[39] the right foot over the left.[40]

"A bowl full of vinegar stood there; so they put a sponge full of the vinegar on hyssop and held it to his mouth" (Jn 19:29). Wine drugged with a grain or two of incense was brought to the prisoner. In actuality, the concoction had no anesthetizing effect, other than psychological.[41]

Hanging on the cross, the criminal would convulse in sudden spasms, throwing his head back and forth. He would have to push himself up with his feet to draw or exhale a breath, and with fatigue the full weight of his body would pull against his wrists. Muscle cramps would knot his forearms, upper arms and shoulders. His pectoral muscles would become paralyzed, except when pushing up against the nail in his feet. Now his legs and thighs would cramp, and he would sag again, his body weight tugging on his nailed wrists.[42]

[36] Ibid., p. 309.
[37] Ibid., p. 311.
[38] Ibid.
[39] Ibid., p. 309.
[40] Ibid., p. 312.
[41] Ibid., p. 310.
[42] Ibid., p. 313.

The cause of death of a crucified man is asphyxiation. There is also considerable loss of blood, in Jesus' case not only because of the crucifixion, but also because of the hematidrosis, the scourging, and the thorns pressed into his scalp. Moreover, he would have been given no food or drink since the evening before, some fourteen hours earlier. He would have experienced a profound thirst, while his body would have been moist from head to toe.[43]

For my part, simply getting a charley horse is a brutal enough reminder to me of what kind of anguish the Savior must have endured in dying for us. But Saint Alphonsus is quick to point out that simply brooding over Jesus' suffering is a fruitless enterprise in itself:

> In thinking on the Passion of our Lord, we should consider not so much the sorrows and insults which he suffered as the love with which he bore them; for Jesus Christ wished to submit to such torments, not only to save us (since for our salvation a single petition offered by him to his Father would be sufficient), but also to make us understand the affection which he entertained for us, and thus gain our hearts.[44]

Forgiveness: proof of God's love for us

A participant in one of the missions I preached wrote on the back of the envelope she used for her offering:

> Thank you for your mission. Please preach and teach about self-forgiveness in your next mission. Fifty years ago I had an abortion. I confessed this mortal sin, but I cannot

---

[43] Ibid., p. 318.

[44] Alphonsus Liguori, "Simple Exposition of the Passion", in *The Passion and the Death of Jesus Christ*, vol. 5 of *The Complete Works of Saint Alphonsus de Liguori*, ed. Rev. Eugene Grimm, C.Ss.R. (Brooklyn, N.Y.: Redemptorist Fathers, 1927), p. 162.

forgive myself. Please help. We do know that the Lord loves sinners. Can he love someone like me?

The answer to her question, of course, is that God does love the sinner, even the sinner who has had an abortion or committed any other serious sin. That is the whole point of the story of Jesus' death on the cross.

In the Gospel of Luke Jesus is anointed by a woman who had once been a prostitute. He says, "Therefore I tell you, her sins, which are many, are forgiven; for she loved much; but he who is forgiven little, loves little" (Lk 7:47).

And Saint Peter Chrysologus, Archbishop of Ravenna, Italy, in the fifth century, says we are actually more beloved in God's sight because of repentance than we could ever be despised by him because of sin: "Before the Heavenly Father, a child rises higher because of pardon than he fell low because of guilt."[45]

Our situation with God is like that of a teenager who is hauled into court to answer at a hearing for some crime. All the evidence is against him, and it is his misfortune that his case is assigned to a defense lawyer who is new in the practice. The young lawyer bungles the case badly and is unable to provide a good defense for the boy. It comes time for a verdict to be rendered by the judge. The judge pronounces: "Case dismissed." All are astounded as they file out of the court. Only the boy, the defense lawyer, and the judge remain. The defense lawyer thinks he has done a good job after all and expects deep thanks from the boy. Instead, he sees the boy go up to the judge and whisper, "Thanks, Dad."

As Saint Paul wrote, "Who shall bring any charge against God's elect? It is God who justifies; who is to condemn?

---

[45] Peter Chrysologus, Sermon 3.

Is it Christ Jesus, who died, yes, who was raised from the dead, who is at the right hand of God, who indeed intercedes for us?" (Rom 8:33–34).

The meaning of redemption

The more I became convinced of God's love for us, especially during those early years of theology studies at the major seminary in Oconomowoc, Wisconsin, the more difficult it was for me to understand why God the Father would demand his Son's death. Yet somehow Jesus' death on the cross and our forgiveness are tied together. Saint Paul has no difficulty in using the Old Testament terminology of sacrifice and expiation to say that Jesus' death brings about our salvation: "In him we have redemption through his blood, the forgiveness of our trespasses, according to the riches of his grace which he lavished upon us" (Eph 1:7–8). Saint John as well sees a connection between Jesus' death and our forgiveness: "[H]e is the expiation for our sins, and not for ours only but also for the sins of the whole world" (1 Jn 2:2). This is the notion of redemption: there is a price to pay for sin, and Jesus pays this price for us. Still I could not understand how a loving Father could demand such a thing of his Son.

Over the years, while not denying the biblical teaching on expiation, I've found a simple way to look at redemption that makes sense to my limited intelligence. This way of looking at it comes down to seeing Jesus' death on the cross as evidence that the Father is patient with us. And we see Jesus' Resurrection from the dead as the basis of hope for our own resurrection and eternal life.

The patience of God

On the night before he died, Jesus celebrated the Paschal supper with his disciples.

> Now as they were eating, Jesus took bread, and blessed,
> and broke it, and gave it to the disciples and said, "Take,
> eat; this is my body." And he took a chalice, and when
> he had given thanks he gave it to them, saying, "Drink
> of it, all of you; for this is my blood of the covenant,
> which is poured out for many for the forgiveness of sins."
> (Mt 26:26–28)

The words of Jesus were probably unfathomable to the
disciples seated with him. They must have wondered what
he meant by saying that the bread in his hands and the cup
of wine before him were his Body and Blood.

It was not the first time that Jesus' words were a mystery
to them. They were used to waiting for his meaning to
become clear. The mystery itself of just who Jesus was had
only recently been clarified for them. Only a week before
this supper, Jesus had asked his disciples: "Who do you
say that I am?" Simon Peter was able to say, "You are the
Christ, the Son of the living God" (Mt 16:15–16).

An event beyond the apostles' comprehension occurred
within hours of the supper. Jesus had eaten the supper
with his apostles on Thursday. The next day, Friday, people committed what Pope John Paul II described as "the
greatest sin that man could commit: the killing of Jesus,
the Son of God, consubstantial with the Father!"[46]

We can assume the apostles were frightened, knowing
the enormity of what had transpired. They were familiar
with the Old Testament concept of a vengeful and jealous
God: "I the LORD your God am a jealous God, visiting the
iniquity of the fathers upon the children to the third and
the fourth generation of those who hate me" (Ex 20:5). If
God had destroyed the world in the time of Noah for what
were more-or-less normal depravities, what would he do

[46]John Paul II, *On the Holy Spirit in the Life of the Church and the World*, 31.

now that people had committed the worst sin that could ever be committed: killing his Son? The apostles may have rightly expected the end of the world as a consequence. In reading Matthew's account of the death of Jesus, one almost senses the expectation that the dreaded Day of the Lord was about to fall on the world.

The prophet Amos had said, "Woe to you who desire the day of the LORD! Why would you have the day of the LORD? It is darkness, and not light" (Amos 5:18). And Matthew describes the darkness settling over the scene of Jesus' death:

> Now from the sixth hour there was darkness over all the land until the ninth hour.... And Jesus cried again with a loud voice and yielded up his spirit. And behold, the curtain of the temple was torn in two, from top to bottom; and the earth shook, and the rocks were split; the tombs also were opened, and many bodies of the saints who had fallen asleep were raised. (Mt 27:45, 50–52)

The events that were taking place were all too similar to what people expected the end of the world to be like.

In fact, in response to the savagery of the murder of his Son, God the Father had only two choices: to punish or to forgive. As we have seen, the only adequate punishment for such an enormous crime would have been to destroy the world. But the fact that we are still here proves that God chose the other alternative: to forgive. Perhaps the apostles recalled the rest of what Jesus had said at the Last Supper: "[T]his is my blood of the covenant, which is poured out for many for the forgiveness of sins" (Mt 26:28).

In every age some people will say they are convinced that the end of the world is coming soon. They say they see so much violence and so many of man's infidelities toward God that surely God will not tolerate this kind of behavior much longer. Yet if God were ever to end the world out of anger, it would have been in response to the murder of his Son. Rather than focus on divine anger, the apostle Peter urges us: "count the forbearance of our Lord as salvation" (2 Pet 3:15).

If God forgave the greatest sin that could ever occur in human history—the murder of his Son Jesus—will he not pardon sins that are less? He certainly will. And all other sins are of less gravity than the murder of the Son of God. So we can say that the lesson we learn from the patience of God the Father in view of the murder committed against his Son is that God forgives all our sins.

Hope for eternal life

The death of Jesus offered God the Father a further opportunity to reveal just how much he loves us. He uses the occasion of Jesus' death to show us what life after death will be like for us.

After his Resurrection, Jesus proved to his disciples that he was not a ghost: "See my hands and my feet, that it is I myself; handle me and see; for a spirit has not flesh and bones as you see that I have" (Lk 24:39). He asked for food to assure them that his body was real. A ghost, if there were such a thing, would not be capable of eating, because it would have no digestive system. "And while they still disbelieved for joy, and wondered, he said to them, 'Have you anything here to eat?' They gave him a piece of broiled fish, and he took it and ate before them" (Lk 24:41–43).

Jesus is risen, soul and body, with powers we can only imagine:

- Jesus can go through closed doors: "The doors were shut, but Jesus came and stood among them" (Jn 20:26).
- Jesus can be in several places at once: "Then he appeared to more than five hundred brethren at one time" (1 Cor 15:6).
- He can float through the air: "[H]e was lifted up, and a cloud took him out of their sight" (Acts 1:9).
- Jesus' humanity has been so perfected that his friends do not recognize him by his facial features; they know who he is only by the nail marks in his hands and feet, which he retains for the purpose of identifying himself: "See my hands and my feet, that it is I myself" (Lk 24:39).

The purpose, then, of Jesus' Resurrection is to give us hope and some insight into what eternal life means for us. The Resurrection of Jesus assures us that God intends that we will be able to enjoy this same resurrected bodily life: "[H]e who eats my flesh and drinks my blood has eternal life, and I will raise him up at the last day" (Jn 6:54).

Just as the patience of God the Father at the time of the crucifixion of Jesus assures us that God forgives us and that our sins are no obstacle to his love for us, the Resurrection of Jesus assures us that physical death will be no obstacle to our living in God's presence for all eternity and enjoying the fullness of human life:

But we would not have you ignorant, brethren, concerning those who are asleep, that you may not grieve as others do who have no hope. For since we believe that Jesus died and rose again, even so, through Jesus, God will bring with him those who have fallen asleep. (1 Thess 4:13–14)

In one sense, it was not necessary that Jesus die on a cross in order for us to be forgiven. Saint Alphonsus quotes John Chrysostom as having said, "One prayer would have been enough to redeem us.... "[A prayer] was not sufficient to make known the love that God has for us."[47]

And in one of his homilies Chrysostom said, "Christ won us over when we were his enemies; now that we have become his friends, let us remain so."[48]

"Redemption" has a broader meaning than simply our being forgiven and given hope. Once we are freed from the shackles of sin and the fear of death, there is no limit to our freedom. Pope Paul VI wrote: "As the kernel and center of his Good News, Christ proclaims salvation, this great gift of God which is liberation from everything that oppresses man but which is above all liberation from sin and the Evil One."[49]

No One Loves Us More Than God

In a Christmas letter, missionary Father Harry Thiel, C.Ss.R., working with the Hmong hill people in Thailand, told of "a pagan lad of [his] acquaintance [who] fell in love with twin sisters. 'They were so much alike,' he claimed, 'I couldn't tell them apart. Since I couldn't decide between them, I married them both!'"

In a sense God loves each of us to the ultimate without taking anything away from anyone else. He does not

[47] Alphonsus Liquori, *The Mysteries of the Faith: The Redemption*, trans. Robert A. Coffin, C.Ss.R (London: Burns & Lambert, 1861), p. 84.

[48] John Chrysostom, Homily 76, in *Commentary on Saint John the Apostle and Evangelist, Homilies 48–88*, vol. 41 of The Fathers of the Church, trans. Sr. Thomas Aquinas Goggin, S.C.H., *Fathers of the Church*, vol. 1 (New York: Fathers of the Church, 1960), p. 321.

[49] Paul VI, *On Evangelization in the Modern World*, 9.

decide among us. He chooses us all. Saint Thérèse of Lisieux explains it this way: "The sun's light, that plays on the cedar-trees, plays on each tiny flower as if it were the only one in existence; and in the same way our Lord takes a special interest in each soul, as if there were no other like it."[50]

On one occasion a seminarian asked me if God has favorites. Singling someone out, especially in a community setting, and telling him he is the favorite would not be wise. Parents have to be very careful about that sort of thing. It is not unusual that among their children there may be one whom they favor over the others. But wise parents would never tell their children that one was favored over another and cause conflict among them. So, when the seminarian asked me whether God has favorites, I said that he treats each and every one of us as if each were his favorite.

Just the same, I cherish the special affection I have for some. I consider it a gift. And I want them always to have that gift from me. Such feelings help me to understand what it means to say that God favors us, that he favors me.

Saint Alphonsus said, "Consider, you have no friend nor brother, nor father nor mother, nor spouse nor lover, who loves you more than your God."[51]

---

[50] Thérèse of Lisieux, *Autobiography of St. Thérèse of Lisieux*, trans. Ronald Knox (New York: P.J. Kenedy and Sons, 1958), p. 35.

[51] Alphonsus Liguori, *The Way to Converse Always and Familiarly with God*, p. 392.

4

FRIENDSHIP WITH GOD

What we have seen so far is that friendship with other people teaches us a great deal about how we might cultivate our friendship with God. Saint Augustine said:

> One Spirit was not sent at one time and then a different Spirit sent at another. Nor is there one love for our neighbor which is entirely different from love for God. There do not exist two kinds of love: we love God with the same love with which we love our neighbor.[1]

And we have also seen that we learn the ways of friendship with God or others by noting how others win our love.

Now we can apply the same elements of friendship from our human relationships to our relationship with God.

Faith in God

At its base, faith is accepting the love of a friend and believing in it. It does not mean suspending rational thought. It does mean suspending our doubts and wariness. It means making a commitment to regard the other as a friend.

Helen Keller, who was blind, deaf, and dumb, had to trust in others all her life. Perhaps it was in trusting other

[1] Augustine, Sermon 265, 8.

people that she learned to trust in God. She wrote: "A simple, childlike faith in a Divine Friend solves all the problems that come to us by land or sea."[2]

Dom Thomas Keating, a Trappist monk, gave a good comparison between faith in God and the faith we place in our earthly fathers when we are children:

> Suppose a neighbor's house starts to burn down. His little boy is trapped on the third floor while all the rest of the family have escaped. The father cannot go back into the house to rescue him. He is standing outside under the window and sees him at the window, silhouetted against the flames. He cries out, "Jump! I'll catch you!" The little boy's eyes are filled with smoke, so he cannot see his father or the ground. He is afraid to jump, even though he desperately wants to be saved. The father cries out again, "Jump! Don't be afraid!"
>
> The little boy cries out: "But Daddy, I can't see you!"
> The father calls back: "But I see you! Jump!"
> So the youngster climbs out onto the window sill and jumps. He lands safely in his father's outstretched arms.
>
> This parable points to what faith is. Of course, most of us have yet to arrive in our Father's arms. We are still in our free fall.[3]

Just as in human friendships, we come to understand another by placing our trust in him, so we come to understand God better by placing our trust or faith in him: "Understanding is the reward of faith. Therefore, seek not to understand that you may believe, but believe that you may understand."[4]

[2] Helen Keller, *My Religion* (San Diego: Book Tree, 2007), p. 185.
[3] Thomas Keating, *The Heart of the World* (New York: Crossroad, 1981), p. 40.
[4] Augustine, *Homilies on the Gospel of John*, 29, 6.

The *Catechism* says, "Faith is man's response to God, who reveals himself and gives himself to man, at the same time bringing man a superabundant light as he searches for the ultimate meaning of his life" (26).

And the *Catechism* emphasizes how important reading the Sacred Scriptures is to nourishing our faith, for how can we place our trust in God if we don't have confidence in his Word? It is also important to pray for the gift of faith and to act in our daily lives with faith. "To live, grow, and persevere in the faith until the end we must nourish it with the word of God; we must beg the Lord to increase our faith;[5] it must be 'working through charity,' abounding in hope, and rooted in the faith of the Church" (162).[6]

Presence

We have seen that an essential element of friendship is the opportunity for friends to be together frequently. But how can we experience God's presence to us? And how can we be present to him?

God's Presence with Us

The stronger the friendship, the greater the desire to see the friend: "Love cannot stand not to see what it loves", said Saint Peter Chrysologus.[7] But where do we "see" God?

The great saints were aware that God is always with us: "As birds, wherever they fly, always are surrounded by air,

[5] Cf. Mk 9:24; Lk 17:5; 22:32.
[6] Gal 5:6; Rom 15:13; cf. Jas 2:14–26.
[7] Peter Chrysologus, Sermon 147.

so we, wherever we go or wherever we are, always find God present",[8] said Saint Francis de Sales.

Saint Teresa described God as present to us in the way water is present to a sponge: "One time I understood how the Lord was present in all things, and how in the soul, and I thought of the example of a sponge which absorbs water."[9]

And Saint Alphonsus said: "Friends in the world have some hours in which they converse together, and others during which they are apart; but between God and you, if you wish, there shall never be one hour of separation."[10]

Saint Teresa of Avila said we could recollect ourselves in the presence of God at any moment:

> When one is in the midst of business matters, and in times of persecutions and trials, when one can't maintain so much quietude, and in times of dryness, Christ is a very good friend because we behold him as man and see him with weaknesses and trials—and he is company for us. Once we have the habit, it is very easy to find him present at our side, although there will come times when neither the one experience nor the other will be possible.[11]

People have told me that they like to pray when they are fishing or out for a walk or in other moments of quiet. In such times, they find it easy to talk to the Lord.

[8] Francis de Sales, *Introduction to the Devout Life*, ed. Msgr. C. Dollen (New York: Alba House, 1992), p. 45.

[9] Teresa of Avila, *Spiritual Testimonies*, I, 40.

[10] Cf. Alphonsus de Liguori, *The Way to Converse Always and Familiarly with God*, in *The Way of Salvation and Perfection*, vol. 2 of *The Complete Works of Saint Alphonsus de Liguori*, ed. Rev. Eugene Grimm, C.Ss.R. (Brooklyn, N.Y.: Redemptorist Fathers, 1926), p. 397.

[11] Teresa of Avila, *The Book of Her Life*, vol. 1 of *The Collected Works of St. Teresa of Avila*, trans. Kieran Kavanaugh, O.C.D., and Otilio Rodriguez, O.C.D. (Washington, D.C.: ICS Publications, 1976), p. 148.

Saint Alphonsus said:

> By reason of his immensity, our God is in every place; but there are two places above all where he has his own peculiar dwelling. One is the highest heaven, where he is present by that glory which he communicates to the blessed; the other is upon earth—it is within the humble soul that loves him: "On high I dwell, and in holiness, and with the crushed and dejected in spirit, to revive the spirits of the dejected, to revive the hearts of the crushed" (Is 57:15).[12]

In the friendship that I enjoy with certain individuals, I have no trouble remembering them and in some sense keeping them present to me, at least in mind. It is a consolation to do so. Thomas à Kempis says in *The Imitation of Christ* that everyone has a need to do the same with Christ: "When Jesus is near, all is well and nothing seems difficult. When he is absent, all is hard."[13] And he warns:

> How dry and hard you are without Jesus! How foolish and vain if you desire anything but him! Is it not a greater loss than losing the whole world? For what, without Jesus, can the world give you? Life without him is a relentless hell, but living with him is a sweet paradise. If Jesus be with you, no enemy can harm you.[14]

Meister Eckehart, a medieval teacher of the spiritual life, said somewhere that we learn to read and write only gradually. It takes a great deal of practice. Initially, we painstakingly trace each letter one by one. Eventually, writing

---

[12] Alphonsus de Liguori, *The Way to Converse Always and Familiarly with God*, pp. 396–97.

[13] Thomas à Kempis, *The Imitation of Christ*, 2, 8.

[14] Ibid.

becomes second nature to us, and we are able to express anything we want in writing, whether trivial things or things that take great courage to put in writing.

Eckehart said that in a similar way a person only gradually becomes accustomed to sensing the presence of God within himself. The person comes to recognize reality for what it is. He does not become entangled merely in material things. But to get to that point, he must proceed slowly and cautiously.

Saint Alphonsus taught the members of his congregation to become attentive to the presence of God by using in the mission house a clock that would chime every quarter hour. He asked his fellow Redemptorists to say a brief prayer recalling God's presence every time they heard the clock chime. Eventually they became continually aware of God's presence.

Our Presence to God

If God is always present to us, Saint Alphonsus says, we should make ourselves consciously present to him:

> Does God love you? Love him. His delights are to be with you; let yours be to be with him, to pass all your lifetime with him, in the delight of whose company you hope to spend a blissful eternity. Accustom yourself to speak with him alone, familiarly, with confidence and love, as to the dearest friend you have, and who loves you best.[15]

Saint Teresa thought it would do the greatest good if people would spend a couple of hours a day placing themselves in God's presence:

---

[15] Alphonsus de Liguori, *The Way to Converse Always and Familiarly with God*, p. 395.

I do not know, my Creator, why it is that everyone does not strive to reach you through this special friendship, and why those who are wicked, who are not conformed to your will, do not, in order that you make them good, allow you to be with them at least two hours each day, even though they may not be with you, but with a thousand disturbances from worldly cares and thoughts, as was the case with me.[16]

We Catholics have a special opportunity to spend time in our Lord's presence by having the gift of the Blessed Sacrament in our churches and chapels. Those who live the consecrated life of a religious brother or sister may at any time sit before our Lord present in the chapel in the house in which they live.

I have had a fairly good relationship with most of the students and novices with whom I have worked. But I appreciated how some would go out of their way to come by my office. They did not have any particular business to settle; they just acknowledged my presence by coming to visit me. Some would simply duck their head in the door to say hello, and occasionally one would pull up a chair to chat for a while.

Jesus would be delighted if you were to stop in at a church or a chapel for a short visit from time to time and especially if you stayed to chat with him for a while. In our postulancy house a student might work on his homework in the chapel. I saw the same when I visited the small chapel, the Portiuncula, or "Port", as the students call it, on the grounds of Franciscan University in Steubenville, Ohio. Those students may have been thinking about their homework, but by working on it in the chapel, they intended to make themselves present to the Lord even though their minds had to be elsewhere.

[16] Teresa of Avila, *The Book of Her Life*, 8, 6.

Saint Alphonsus, who was always looking for a practical way to encourage people in their spiritual life, wrote *Visits to the Blessed Sacrament*, in which he scripted conversations for people to have with Christ in the presence of the Blessed Sacrament. While visits to the Blessed Sacrament were not part of the life of the apostles, so far as we know, nor part of the life of the early Church, it seems to be a logical development from our belief in the Real Presence of Christ in the Blessed Sacrament. If he is there in a special way, why not visit him in a special way?

Prayer: Conversation with God

Three treasure hunters discovered in a castle a hidden room where they were sure there must be great amounts of treasure stored, since it was secured by a lock that could not be opened. They found, however, that by squeezing through a small hole they made in the wall and crawling with difficulty through a series of shafts, they could make their way into the room. The treasure there exceeded their wildest imaginings: great hoards of diamonds and rubies, gold and silver. But the door to the room was impossible to budge from the inside as well. So the treasure hunters made their way out of the treasury with as much as they could carry or drag behind them, knowing that the narrow spaces through which they had to crawl would not permit them to take much loot. After two of these treasure hunters had left, however, the third took from his pocket one more item that he had not shown the others, his most important find in the whole treasury. It was the key to the lock on the great door of the treasure room. With it he could go in and out whenever he pleased.

Prayer is the key to the treasures of the spiritual life. Conversation between friends is vital for the growth of a friendship, whether with a human friend or with God.

Saint Teresa of Avila's definition of prayer emphasizes not word but mutual presence. For her, prayer is "an intimate sharing between friends; it means taking time frequently to be alone with him who we know loves us".[17]

Teresa's namesake, Thérèse of Lisieux, also could communicate with the Lord without many words: "For me, prayer is a surge of the heart; it is a simple look turned toward heaven, it is a cry of recognition and of love, embracing both trial and joy."[18]

These saints knew that the love of the heart was far more important than the words on the lips. As the *Catechism* teaches: "Love is the source of prayer; whoever draws from it reaches the summit of prayer" (2658). When I have been away long from friends whom I love very much, I can anticipate that the next time I see them, the joy on my face will communicate more to them than any words I can speak.

But in prayer we do have the opportunity to express ourselves in words. Saint John Damascene, a Father of the Church whose life bridged the last half of the seventh century and the first half of the eighth, said: "Prayer is the raising of one's mind and heart to God or the requesting of good things from God."[19]

Saint Alphonsus encouraged us to request favors from God:

---

[17] Teresa of Avila, *The Book of Her Life*, 8, 5.

[18] Thérèse of Lisieux, *Manuscrits autobiographiques*, C 25r, quoted in *Catechism of the Catholic Church*, 2558.

[19] John of Damascene, *De fide orthodoxa*, 3, 24: *PG* 94, 1089C, quoted in *Catechism of the Catholic Church*, 2559.

Ask those people who love [God] with a true love, and they will tell you that in the sorrows of their life they find no greater, no truer relief, than in a loving conversation with God.

Now this does not require that you continually apply your mind to it, so as to forget all your tasks and recreations. It only requires of you, without putting these aside, to act toward God as you act on occasion toward those who love you and whom you love.

Your God is ever near you, more so, within you: "In him we live and move and have our being" (Acts 17:28). There is no barrier at the door against any who desire to speak with him; no, rather, God delights that you should deal with him confidently. Treat with him of your business, your plans, your griefs, your fears—of all that concerns you. Above all, do so (as I have said) with confidence, with open heart. For God is not wont to speak to the soul that speaks not to him; forasmuch as, if it be not used to converse with him, it would little understand his voice when he spoke to it.[20]

Saint Francis de Sales recommended frequent little comments thrown up to God:

Imitate little children walking with their father. They keep one hand in his and with the other pick the strawberries and currants along the way. Attend to your work, but every once in a while lift up your mind to your heavenly Father to see whether your work is pleasing to him and to ask his help.[21]

Thomas à Kempis says we need to learn to take moments of prayer:

[20]Alphonsus de Liguori, *The Way to Converse Always and Familiarly with God*, pp. 395–96.

[21]Francis de Sales, quoted in *Spiritual Diary: Selected Sayings and Examples of the Saints* (Boston: St. Paul Editions, 1962), pp. 175–76.

It is a great art to know how to converse with Jesus, and great wisdom to know how to keep him. Be humble and peaceful, and Jesus will be with you. Be devout and calm, and he will remain with you. You may quickly drive him away and lose his grace, if you turn back to the outside world. And, if you drive him away and lose him, to whom will you go and whom will you then seek as a friend?[22]

We pray to God not because he needs to hear our prayers, but because we need to be aware of his concern for us. Our prayers are not for God's instruction but for our own. Saint Alphonsus observed:

Say not, But where is the need of disclosing to God all my wants, if he already sees and knows them better than I? True, he knows them. But God makes as if he knew not the necessities about which you do not speak to him, and for which you seek not his aid. Our Savior knew well that Lazarus was dead, and yet he made as if he knew not, until the Magdalene had told him of it, and then he comforted her by raising her brother to life again.[23]

We should pray not only for our own needs but for those of others as well. Saint Alphonsus tells us:

Use toward [God] also the freedom of recommending not only your own needs, but also those of others. How agreeable will it be to your God that sometimes you forget even your own interests to speak to him of the advancement of his glory, of the miseries of others, especially those who groan in affliction, of those souls, his spouses, who in purgatory sigh after the vision of God himself, and of poor sinners who are living destitute of his grace![24]

[22] Thomas à Kempis, *The Imitation of Christ*, 2, 8.
[23] Cf. Alphonsus de Liguori, *The Way to Converse Always and Familiarly with God*, p. 399.
[24] Ibid., p. 406.

Saint Thomas Aquinas said that our asking a favor of God is only fair since he asks that we do his will: "It is appropriate in the name of reciprocal love that God should do the will of those who do his will, granting their desires and their prayers for others."[25]

Suffering and great need move us to pray, as Saint Alphonsus noted:

> When, therefore, you are afflicted with any sickness, temptation, persecution, or other trouble, go at once and beseech him, that his hand may help you. It is enough for you to present the affliction before him; to come in and say, "Behold, O LORD, for I am in distress" (Lam 1:20). He will not fail to comfort you, or at least to give you strength to suffer that grief with patience; and it will turn out a greater good to you than if he had altogether freed you from it. Tell him all the thoughts of fear or of sadness that torment you; and say to him, "My God, in thee are all my hopes; I offer to thee this affliction, and resign myself to thy will; but do thou take pity on me—either deliver me out of it, or give me strength to bear it. And he will truly keep with you that promise made in the Gospel to all those who are in trouble, to console and comfort them as often as they have recourse to him: "Come to me, all who labor and are heavy laden, and I will give you rest" (Mt 11:28).[26]

God will answer our prayers at the time and in the way he knows is best for us: "Do not be fainthearted in your prayer, nor neglect to give alms" (Sir 7:10). This verse

[25] Thomas Aquinas, quoted in Marie Joseph Nicolas, O.P., "The Obedience of Mary," in *Obedience and the Church* (Washington, D.C.: Corpus Books, 1968), p. 38.

[26] Cf. Alphonsus de Liguori, *The Way to Converse Always and Familiarly with God*, pp. 399–400.

from the Word of God reminds us that there are others looking for help from us just as desperately as we are looking for help from God.

When we looked at human friendships, we said we should be careful to center our conversation on what is important to the person to whom we are speaking. Likewise, in prayer, we should center our attention on what is of interest to God. Although everything is of interest to God, he is especially interested in our love for him. "True prayer is always God-centered; selfish prayer is gift-centered."[27]

Saint Alphonsus especially recommended prayers of gratitude:

> Further, when you receive pleasant news, do not act like those unfaithful, thankless souls who have recourse to God in time of trouble, but in time of prosperity forget and forsake him. Be as faithful to him as you would be to a friend who loves you and rejoices in your good; go at once and tell him of your gladness, and praise him and give him thanks, acknowledging it all as a gift from his hands; and rejoice in that happiness because it comes to you of his good pleasure.[28]

Most of all, Alphonsus says, we should pray frequently so that we will be able to perceive what God is trying to communicate to us:

> In a word, if you desire to delight the loving heart of your God, be careful to speak to him as often as you are able, and with the fullest confidence that he will not disdain to

[27]Johannes Hofinger, S.J., "How to Pray for Healing", Priest 36 (April 1980): 42.

[28]Alphonsus de Liguori, The Way to Converse Always and Familiarly with God, pp. 402–3.

answer and speak with you in return. He does not, indeed, make himself heard in any voice that reaches your ears, but in a voice that your heart can well perceive, when you withdraw from converse with creatures, to occupy yourself in conversing with your God alone: "I will ... bring her into the wilderness, and speak tenderly to her heart" (Hos 2:14). He will then speak to you by such inspirations, such interior lights, such manifestations of his goodness, such sweet touches in your heart, such tokens of forgiveness, such experience of peace, such hopes of heaven, such rejoicings within you, such sweetness of his grace, such loving and close embraces—in a word, such voices of love—as are well understood by those souls whom he loves, and who seek for nothing but himself alone.[29]

Catholic publisher Frank Sheed in his later years seemed to have attained to a contemplative state. Once when Father Benedict Groeschel, a friend of his, walked in on him in Frank's New Jersey apartment, he found the old man leaning forward in his chair.

"Can I get you something to read?" asked the priest.

Frank opened his eyes and said, "Oh heavens, no. I've read it all. I just like to listen."[30]

Father Henri Nouwen, a spiritual writer of the twentieth century, said that we have become unable to hear God or to understand which direction he is telling us to take. He said we live an "absurd" life as a result. The Latin word *surdus* means "deaf". We need to live a more disciplined life, Father Nouwen said, and he pointed out that the Latin word *audire*, "to listen", is the root of our English word "obedience". [31]

---

[29] Ibid., p. 408.

[30] Benedict Groeschel, *Spiritual Passages* (New York: Crossroad, 1983), p. 177.

[31] See Henri J.M. Nouwen, *Making All Things New* (San Francisco: Harper and Row, 1981), p. 67.

All of this is in line with the observation of *The Imitation of Christ*: "When Jesus does not speak within, all other comfort is empty, but if he says only a word, it brings great consolation."[32]

When physical presence to the friend is not possible, at least some form of communication with him or some sort of mutual retention of memories is necessary. As Catholics we cherish the most remarkable remembrance we can have of our Savior. At the Last Supper Jesus gave us himself to be with us in sacramental form, under the guise of bread and wine, until the end of time. "Do this in remembrance of me", Jesus said (Lk 22:19).

Conversely, just because the friend is physically present, we should not assume we are growing in our friendship. In fact, unless there is meaningful communication, friendship will tend to die. Some people attend Mass and receive Communion countless times with so little consciousness of what they do that they not only get nothing out of it but positively do themselves harm by ignoring Christ's presence in the sacrament. "For any one who eats and drinks without discerning the body eats and drinks judgment upon himself" (1 Cor 11:29). Yet the solution is not to go to Communion less but to be more conscious of the Gift whom we receive.

Sin separates us from God even though we may be in a chapel or on our knees. "If our heart is far from God, the words of prayer are in vain" (*CCC* 2562). Yet Saint Alphonsus says that repentance of sin and the desire to improve can be a wonderful experience that moves us closer to God:

By [your] having immediate recourse to God to ask his forgiveness, and to promise him amendment, your very

---

[32] Thomas à Kempis, *The Imitation of Christ*, 2, 8.

faults will serve to advance you further in the divine love. Between friends who sincerely love each other it often happens that when one has displeased the other, and then humbles himself and asks pardon, their friendship thereby becomes stronger than ever. Do you likewise; see to it that your very faults serve to bind you yet closer in love to your God.[33]

Knowing God

Saint Gregory of Nyssa, who lived in the fourth century and was the younger brother of Saint Basil the Great and a friend of Saint Gregory Nazianzen, compares the attempt to know God to the dizzying effect of looking "down into the depths of the sea from the top of a mountain".

Along the seacoast, you may often see mountains facing the sea. It is as though they had been sliced in two, with a sheer drop from top to bottom. At the top a projection forms a ledge overhanging the depth below. If a man were to look down from that ledge he would be overcome by dizziness.... [God] is that smooth, steep, and sheer rock, on which the mind can find no secure resting place to get a grip or lift ourselves up.... Yet God does raise and sustain our flagging hopes. He rescued Peter from drowning and made the sea into a firm surface beneath his feet. He does the same for us; the hands of the Word of God are stretched out to us when we are out of our depth, buffeted and lost in speculation. Grasped firmly in his hands, we shall be without fear: *Blessed are the pure of heart*, [Christ the Word] says, *for they shall see God*."[34]

[33] Cf. Alphonsus de Liguori, *The Way to Converse Always and Familiarly with God*, p. 406.

[34] Gregory of Nyssa, *Orat. 6, De Beatitudinibus* in *The Liturgy of the Hours* (New York: Catholic Book Publishing, 1975), 3:403.

Ultimately, the result of conversation with another person is that we get to know him better. Knowledge of a person comes from spending time with him and especially from listening to him.

"It is not good for a man to be without knowledge, and he who makes haste with his feet misses his way" (Prov 19:2). We can have the best intentions to serve God, but if we do not know God and what he wants from us, we may do just the opposite of giving him our love.

Saint Teresa of Avila told once of a blunder she almost made by admiring what she thought to be virtuous conduct while neglecting to take into account what she knew God expected of her:

> Once while thinking about the severe penance Doña Catalina de Cardona performed and about how because of the desires for penance the Lord sometimes gives me I could have done more were it not for obedience to my confessors, I thought it might be better not to obey them any longer in this matter. The Lord told me: "That's not so; you are walking on a good and safe path. Do you see all the penance she does? I value your obedience more."[35]

The very purpose of the Word of God taking flesh was to reveal to us who God is. The ancient writer Saint Irenaeus taught:

> True knowledge, then, consists in understanding Christ. Paul calls it the wisdom of God hidden in a mystery. [He says:] "The natural person does not accept" (1 Cor 2:14) the doctrine of the cross. A person who "tastes" this doctrine will not give in to the disputations and quibbles of proud and puffed-up people, who go into matters of

[35] Teresa of Avila, *Spiritual Testimonies*, 19.

which they have no perception. For the truth is unsophisticated. And "the word is near you, in your mouth and in your heart" (Rom 10:8; Deut 30:14) as the same apostle declares. It is easy to understand for those who are obedient. For it makes us like Christ, if we experience "the power of his resurrection and the sharing of his sufferings" (Phil 3:10).[36]

So, the Scriptures tell us, "Let us know, let us press on to know the LORD" (Hos 6:3). But there is a big difference between knowing about Christ and knowing Christ. There is a story that says when Saint Thomas Aquinas went to visit his friend Saint Bonaventure, Thomas asked to see the library. Bonaventure pointed to the crucifix on the wall: "There is everything I know", he said.[37]

It is possible to be well instructed about theology without knowing Jesus Christ. Saint Irenaeus comments:

> It is better that a person should have no knowledge whatever of how a single thing in creation has been made, as long as he believes in God and continues in his love, than that, puffed up through knowledge of this kind, he should fall away from that love which is our life. And [it is better] that he should search after no other knowledge except [the knowledge of] Jesus Christ, the Son of God, who was crucified for us, than that by subtle questions and hair-splitting rhetoric he should fall into insulting God.[38]

My experience with people for whom I have felt the strongest affection is that I wanted to know them in order

---

[36] Irenaus, "Fragments from the Lost Writings of St. Irenaeus", 36, in vol. 1 of *Ante-Nicene Fathers*, ed. Alexander Roberts and James Donaldson (Buffalo, N.Y.: Christian Literature Publishers, 1885).

[37] Cf. Robert Payne, *The Fathers of the Western Church* (London: Heinemann, 1952), p. 279.

[38] Irenaeus, *Against Heresies*, 2, 26, 1.

to know whether they had the same level of appreciation and regard for me as I had for them. Saint Francis of Assisi put it this way in a prayer requesting greater love of the Lord: "I wish to know you so that I may come to love you."

Saint Teresa of Avila thought that Martha, the friend of Jesus, may have suffered from the suspicion that Jesus did not really care about her:

> I sometimes remember the complaint of that holy woman, Martha. She did not complain only about her sister, rather, I hold it is certain that her greatest sorrow was the thought that you, Lord, did not feel sad about the trial she was undergoing and didn't care whether she was with you or not. Perhaps she thought you didn't have as much love for her as for her sister. This must have caused her greater sorrow than did serving the one for whom she had such great love; for love turns work into rest. It seems that in saying nothing to her sister but in directing her whole complaint to you, Lord, that love made her dare to ask why you weren't concerned. And even your reply seems to refer to her complaint as I have interpreted it, for love alone is what gives value to all things; and a kind of love so great that nothing hinders it is the one thing necessary.[39]

Sometimes we have to force understanding on ourselves by presuming goodwill on the part of our friend. Saint Gregory the Great, a pope of the sixth century, said, "It is not by faith that you will come to know the Lord, but by love; not by conviction, but by action."[40] It is in taking the chance of loving the Lord that we come to know him.

---

[39] Teresa of Avila, *Soliloquies*, 5, 2.
[40] Gregory the Great, Homily 14, 3–6.

Conversely, we can say that a lack of understanding between individuals is based in a lack of love. It was because Jesus' enemies had no love for him that they simply could not understand him. As he said to them on one occasion: "You know neither me nor my Father; if you knew me, you would know my Father also" (Jn 8:19).

Relationship building takes time and understanding. It was only after a great deal of personal conversion that Saint Paul came to know Christ. "Indeed I count everything as loss because of the surpassing worth of knowing Christ Jesus my Lord. For his sake I have suffered the loss of all things, and count them as refuse, in order that I may gain Christ" (Phil 3:8).

Saint Teresa of Avila talks about an advanced point in the spiritual life in which a person shares an intimate knowledge of God that does not require words or formulation:

> I think that just as in heaven you understand without speaking (which I certainly never knew until the Lord in his goodness desired that I should see and showed himself to me in a rapture), so it is in this vision. For God and the soul understand each other only through the desire his Majesty had that it understand him, without the use of any other means devised to manifest the love these two friends have for each other. It's like the experience of two persons here on earth who love each other deeply and understand each other well; even without signs, just by a glance, it seems, they understand each other.[41]

Realizing the joy of knowing the Lord in love, Pope John Paul II said: "If we are silent about the joy that comes from knowing Jesus, the very stones will cry out!"[42]

[41] Teresa of Avila, *The Book of Her Life*, 27, 10.
[42] Pope John Paul II, quoted in Cal and Rose Samra, *Holy Humor* (Carmel, New York: Guideposts, 1996), p. 60.

Sharing

A friendship is built on sharing between friends. This is also true of friendship with God.

Mutual Benefit

A friendship is particularly valuable and authentic when it has some mutual benefit.

Saint Alphonsus Liguori remarks:

> The Angelic Doctor, Saint Thomas [Aquinas], says that friendship is founded on the mutual communication of goods; for as friendship is nothing more than a mutual love between friends, it follows that there must be a reciprocal interchange of the good that each possesses. Hence the saint says: "If there be no communication, there is no friendship." On this account Jesus Christ says to his disciples: "I have called you friends, because all things whatsoever I have heard of my Father I have made known to you" (Jn 15:15). Since he had made them his friends, he had communicated all his secrets to them.[43]

We, of course, benefit from our friendship with God, as Saint Alphonsus points out:

> Speak to [God] as often as you can; for he does not grow weary of this nor disdain it, as do the lords of the earth. If you love him, you will not be at a loss to know what to say to him. Tell him all that occurs to you about yourself and your affairs, as you would tell it to a dear friend.

---

[43] Cf. Alphonsus de Liguori, *The Practice of the Love of Jesus Christ*, in *The Holy Eucharist*, vol. 6 of *The Complete Works of Saint Alphonsus de Liguori: The Ascetical Works*, ed. Rev. Eugene Grimm, C.Ss.R. (New York: Benziger Brothers, 1887), p. 439.

Look not upon him as a haughty sovereign, who will only converse with the great, and on great matters. He, our God, delights to abase himself to converse with us, loves to have us communicate to him our smallest, our most daily concerns. He loves you as much, and has as much care for you, as if he had no others to think of but yourself. He is as entirely devoted to your interests as though the only end of his providence were to succor you, of his almighty power to aid you, of his mercy and goodness to take pity on you, to do you good, and to gain by the delicate touches of his kindness your confidence and love.[44]

What benefit does God get from our friendship? It seems God wants only our love. And yet, even if we were successful in loving God completely, we could never out-love him. Saint Teresa of Avila shows that even as God receives love from his creature, he gives still more love:

And the more our deeds show that these are not merely polite words, all the more does the Lord bring us to himself and raise the soul from itself and all earthly things so as to make it capable of receiving great favors, for he never finishes repaying this service in the present life. He esteems it so highly that we do not ourselves know how to ask for ourselves, and his Majesty never tires of giving. Not content with having made this soul one with himself, he begins to find his delight in it, reveal his secrets, and rejoice that it knows what it has gained and something of what he will give it. He makes it lose these exterior senses so that nothing will occupy it. This is rapture. And he begins to commune with the soul in so intimate a friendship that he not only gives it back its own will but gives it his. For in so great a friendship the Lord takes joy

---

[44] Cf. Alphonsus de Liguori, *The Way to Converse Always and Familiarly with God*, pp. 398–99.

in putting the soul in command, as they say, and he does what it asks since it does his will. And he does this even better than the soul itself could, for he is powerful and does whatever he wants and never stops wanting this.[45]

Similar Traits

In human friendships, friends share similar interests and even come to resemble each other. Following the advice of the Scriptures, we become more like God as we are merciful and loving toward God's children. Jesus said, "Be merciful, even as your Father is merciful" (Lk 6:36), and "A disciple is not above his teacher, but every one when he is fully taught will be like his teacher" (Lk 6:40). Saint Paul advises us: "Therefore be imitators of God, as beloved children. And walk in love, as Christ loved us and gave himself up for us, a fragrant offering and sacrifice to God" (Eph 5:1–2).

There is a story from ancient Greece of a magician who tried to imitate God by conjuring up a threatening storm:

[Salmoneus] pretended that he was Zeus. He had a chariot made in such a way that there was a loud clanging of brass when it moved. On the day of Zeus' festival he drove it furiously through the town, scattering at the same time fire-brands and shouting to the people to worship him because he was Zeus the Thunderer. But instantly there came a crash of actual thunder and a flash of lightning. Salmoneus fell from his chariot dead.[46]

---

[45] Teresa of Avila, *The Way of Perfection*, in *The Way of Perfection, Meditation on the Song of Songs, The Interior Castle*, vol. 2 of *The Collected Works of St. Teresa of Avila*, trans. Kieran Kavanaugh, O.C.D., and Otilio Rodriguez, O.C.D. (Washington, D.C.: ICS Publications, 1980), p. 164.

[46] Edith Hamilton, *Mythology* (Boston: Little, Brown, 1969), p. 298.

We would not use Salmoneus' approach to imitate God. We imitate God by practicing virtue, as the letter of the Church Father Mathetes to Diognetus confirms:

> Don't be surprised that someone can imitate God. Anyone may who wishes to do so. However, it is not by having the upper hand over others, or by being more powerful than others, or by having more wealth, or by forcing others to do our bidding. That is not what makes us happy and that is not what makes us imitators of God. What makes a person an imitator of God is taking on the burdens that others carry, using what we have to help others, being generous with what we have received from God—these are the things that make us imitators of God.[47]

Nor should we imagine that our growth in likeness to Christ is something we can simply ascribe to ourselves. Saint Thérèse of Lisieux cautions us:

> Perfection has nothing to do with receiving a whole lot of lights in prayer! ... To other people, of course, they may be very useful; people who are humble enough to thank God for letting them share in such a treat, and for enriching a soul with such dainties. But the person so enriched mustn't take credit to herself for these profitable thoughts, plume herself on them like the Pharisee in the temple. That would be like a man dying of hunger in full sight of his own well-stocked table, while his guests, helping themselves generously, looked round with envy at a man who was so well off![48]

---

[47] *Letter of Mathetes to Diognetus*, 10.

[48] Thérèse of Lisieux, *Autobiography of St. Thérèse of Lisieux*, trans. Ronald Knox (New York: P.J. Kenedy and Sons, 1958), p. 278.

Thérèse is saying that the more we pride ourselves on the gifts of holiness that God shares with us, the less holy we will be.

Communion with God

The goal of friendship is to establish a bond with the friend. This is also true of our communion with Jesus. As the *Catechism* states, "Man is made to live in communion with God in whom he finds happiness: 'When I am completely united to you, there will be no more sorrow or trials; entirely full of you, my life will be complete'" (45).[49]

Jesus talked about the bond we have with him and the Father: "Yet a little while, and the world will see me no more, but you will see me; because I live, you will live also. In that day you will know that I am in my Father, and you in me, and I in you" (Jn 14:19–20).

Saint Irenaeus wrote: "God, who stands in need of no one, gave communion with himself to those in need of him."[50] And Saint Gregory the Great said in a homily on the Gospels, "We hold in our hearts One we have not seen in the flesh."[51]

The *Catechism* says that everyone is called to communion with Christ and that some people have a unique experience of mystical union with Christ:

Spiritual progress tends toward ever more intimate union with Christ. This union is called "mystical" because it participates in the mystery of Christ through the

[49] Augustine, *Confessions*, 10, 28, 39: *PL* 32.
[50] Irenaeus, *Against Heresies*, 4, 14, 2.
[51] Gregory the Great, Homily 26, 9.

sacraments—"the holy mysteries"—and, in him, in the mystery of the Holy Trinity. God calls us all to this intimate union with him, even if the special graces of extraordinary signs of this mystical life are granted only to some for the sake of manifesting the gratuitous gift given to all. (2014)

Thérèse of Lisieux was one of those who appreciated the deep communion she had with Christ. She talked about her First Communion (at age eleven):

What comfort it brought to me, that first kiss our Lord imprinted on my soul! A lover's kiss; I knew that I was loved, and I, in my turn, told him that I loved him, and was giving myself to him for all eternity. It was a long time now since he had made any demands on me; there had been no struggles, no sacrifices; we had exchanged looks, he and I, insignificant though I was, and we had understood one another. And now it wasn't a question of looks; something had melted away, and there were no longer two of us—Thérèse had simply disappeared, like a drop lost in the ocean; Jesus only was left, my Master, my King.[52]

Recall that common experiences, common values, mutual interest, and mutual respect help establish the communion of friendship, and the more intimate the bond, the deeper the friendship will be.

When friends tell me, "We think alike", I usually reply kiddingly, "It's scary, isn't it?" But they are trying to say that in thinking alike we have a common bond.

The bond we have with Jesus is even more intimate. As the *Catechism* says: "To receive communion is to receive Christ himself who has offered himself for us" (1382).

---

[52] Thérèse of Lisieux, *Autobiography of St. Thérèse of Lisieux*, pp. 105–6.

Saint Alphonsus offers this comparison:

As fire penetrates iron, and seems to change it into itself, so does God penetrate the soul and fill her with himself; and though she never loses her own being, yet she becomes so penetrated and absorbed by that immense ocean of the divine substance, that she remains, as it were anni-hilated, and as if she ceased to exist. The Apostle [Saint Paul] prayed for this happy lot for his disciples when he said: "that you may be filled with all the fulness of God" (Eph 3:19).[53]

The medieval monk and mystic Meister Eckehart described how deeply a person identifies with God because of his communion with Christ. Anyone who touches a person who is in communion with Christ touches God in effect because God surrounds the person as a monk's robes surround the monk. Meister Eckehart also said that when we eat something bitter, it affects our taste, because food and drink pass over our tongue. Likewise, the person who is in deep communion with Christ is surrounded by Christ. Anything affecting his life must come through Christ to him and be experienced in a Christlike way. So, we experience our sorrows as Christ experienced his sor-rows. Negatives become positives: insults become hon-ors; bitterness becomes sweetness; deep darkness becomes bright light. Whatever such a person who lives in union with Christ experiences becomes a divine experience, sor-row becoming ecstasy.

Luis de León was a Spanish Augustinian monk of the sixteenth century. He described a cloud that was radiated by the sun's rays and glowed with the sun's brightness and

[53] Alphonsus de Liguori, *The Practice of the Love of Jesus Christ*, p. 446.

said that, in a similar way, the person united with Christ is filled with Christ's virtue, light, body, and Spirit. Christ's Spirit mingles with the spirit of that kind of person united with him. Christ's body is absorbed into the body of such a one. As a consequence, it is Christ who peers through the eyes of the person in communion with him. Christ speaks and works through him. The person's face and actions reflect the face and actions of Christ because Christ is so thoroughly united to him.

We saw earlier that to have a deep bond with another person, we must reveal a great deal about ourselves. Often this sharing happens over meals. Before a friend of mine was to move to another part of the country, he invited me to have breakfast with him at a restaurant. I was grateful for the invitation because the breakfast gave us a final opportunity to be together as friends.

I see that as the impact that the Eucharist has on us. It is, after all, the Lord's Last Supper. Somehow, in the mystery that envelops God, we experience that Supper with Jesus every time we celebrate the Eucharist. Somehow we step over the threshold from time into eternity. The Lord's Supper is the doorframe. In it are the birth, death, and Resurrection of the Lord as well as every celebration of the Eucharist that has happened or will happen on Earth. In the Eucharist we are joined with the angels and saints in the eternal liturgy of worship offered to the Father in heaven.

The Lord becomes sacramentally present to us in the Eucharist, and his Real Presence remains in the tabernacle after our gathering. His is the presence of a Friend with whom we can spend time and talk. We have him present within us as we have him present before us. In 1898, while he was still studying theology in the seminary, the future Pope John XXIII wrote in his personal journal, "In the Blessed Sacrament I will be united with Jesus, my friend and comforter, and all will be well."[54]

Saint Teresa of Avila described what she came to understand as communion with God:

> In explaining the nature of union to me, [the Lord] said: "Don't think, daughter, that union lies in being very close to me. For those, too, who offend me are close, although they may not want to be. Neither does it consist in favors and consolations in prayer, even though these may reach a very sublime degree. Though these favors may come from me, they are often a means for winning souls, even souls that are not in the state of grace."
>
> I understood that [union] consists in the spirit being pure and raised above all earthly things so that there is nothing in the soul that wants to turn aside from God's will; but there is such conformity with God in spirit and will, and detachment from everything, and involvement with him, that there is no thought of love of self or of any creature.[55]

Sacrifice for God's Sake

I welcome opportunities to make sacrifices for friends. Jesus said there is no greater love than to lay down one's life for a friend (see Jn 15:13).

In Thomas à Kempis' *Imitation of Christ*, Jesus says, "I seek not your gift but you."[56]

Jesus told us that our love for him must come even before our love for family members or our desire to cling to our own life:

[54] John XXIII, *Journal of a Soul*, trans. Dorothy White (New York: McGraw-Hill, 1965), p. 20.

[55] Teresa of Avila, *Spiritual Testimonies*, 25, 1 and 2.

[56] Thomas à Kempis, *Imitation of Christ*, 4, 8.

He who loves father or mother more than me is not worthy of me; and he who loves son or daughter more than
me is not worthy of me; and he who does not take his
cross and follow me is not worthy of me. He who finds
his life will lose it, and he who loses his life for my sake
will find it. (Mt 10:37–39)

Once I was teaching religion to a group of teenagers
when the question of martyrdom came up. Not a single
student saw the purpose of laying down one's life for his
faith. Each of these Christian young people declared that
he would conform to whatever was asked of him by a per-
secutor rather than give up his life.

The bishops of the Second Vatican Council reminded
us that martyrdom is the supreme testimony and act of
loyalty of a disciple of Christ:

Since Jesus, the Son of God, manifested His charity by
laying down His life for us, so too no one has greater love
than he who lays down his life for Christ and his brothers
(cf. 1 Jn 3:16; Jn 15:13). From the earliest times, then,
some Christians have been called upon—and some will
always be called upon—to give this supreme testimony
of this love to all men, but especially to persecutors. The
Church, then, considers martyrdom as an exceptional gift
and as the fullest proof of love. By martyrdom a disciple is
transformed into an image of his Master, by freely accepting death for the salvation of the world—as well as his
conformity to Christ in the shedding of his blood. Though
few are presented such an opportunity, nevertheless all
must be prepared to confess Christ before men. They must
be prepared to make this profession of faith even in the
midst of persecutions, which will never be lacking to
the Church, in following the way of the Cross.[57]

[57] Vatican II, Dogmatic Constitution on the Church (*Lumen Gentium*), 42.

Do we need to remind ourselves that Jesus first of all offered his life as a sacrifice for us? "For Christ, our Paschal Lamb, has been sacrificed" (1 Cor 5:7). The sacrifice of Jesus for us should inspire us to sacrifice ourselves for him and for others: "By this we know love, that he laid down his life for us; and we ought to lay down our lives for the brethren" (1 Jn 3:16).

The way we sometimes complain about the sacrifices we have to make may cause people to think we need not have bothered! Saint Teresa of Avila said, "Learn to suffer something for the love of God, without letting everyone know about it."[58]

And Saint Gregory points out that the truly generous person who is called upon to make a sacrifice on behalf of others does not pity himself for it but is solicitous about the needs of others. Even more so would the holy person want his Lord to be well served:

> It is characteristic of holy men that their own painful trials do not make them lose their concern for the well-being of others. They are grieved by the adversity they must endure, yet they look out for others and teach them needed lessons; they are like gifted physicians who are themselves stricken and lie ill. They suffer wounds themselves but bring others the medicine that restores health.[59]

Jesus has told us that sacrifice for his sake is not without its rewards:

> Peter began to say to him, "Behold, we have left everything and followed you." Jesus said, "Truly, I say to you,

---

[58] Teresa of Avila, quoted in *Spiritual Diary*, p. 95.

[59] Gregory the Great, *Moral Reflections*, 3, 40, in *The Liturgy of the Hours*, 4:127.

there is no one who has left house or brothers or sisters or mother or father or children or lands, for my sake and for the gospel, who will not receive a hundredfold now in this time, houses and brothers and sisters and mothers and children and lands, with persecutions, and in the age to come eternal life." (Mk 10:28–30)

I find this passage especially consoling when I think I have given up a great deal to become a priest and religious. But I would be further along in the spiritual life if I could think of the sacrifices I am called to make as acts of love. And to be able to love God is reward enough.

Loyalty to God in Spite of Suffering

Recall that communion with a friend must be not only deep but also enduring. Loyalty to the friend is an essential element of authentic friendship.

It is also true of our relationship with God. Saint John Chrysostom said that we should look first to Christ to see how he modeled loyalty to his Father in spite of his sufferings:

In case [Jesus' disciples] might say: "We have fallen from the Father's favor, we have been abandoned and have become deserted and stripped of all things," he said: "Look at me; I am loved by my Father, but nevertheless I shall endure the sufferings that now lie before me. Well, then, I am not forsaking you either, nor am I leaving you because I do not love you. For, if I am slain and yet do not count this a proof of not being loved by the Father, you ought not to be disturbed either. If you abide in my love, these evils will lack power to harm you in proportion to your love."[60]

Saint Alphonsus also advised humble loyalty, even when in our spirit we have no verve to continue:

And when the desolation lasts long, and troubles you exceedingly, unite your voice to that of Jesus in agony and dying on the Cross, and beseech his mercy, saying, "My God, my God, why have you forsaken me?" (Mt 27:46). But let the effect of this be to humble you yet more at the thought that he deserves no consolations who has offended God; and yet more to enliven your confidence, knowing that God does all things, and permits all, for your good: "We know that in everything God works for good with those who love him, who are called according to his purpose" (Rom 8:28).[61]

Friendship is a commitment. In that sense, it is an act of faith. "By this we shall know that we are of the truth, and reassure our hearts before him whenever our hearts condemn us; for God is greater than our hearts, and he knows everything" (1 Jn 3:19–20).

Patience

We saw earlier that to remain loyal to a friend sometimes requires extraordinary patience. Saint Augustine said in

---

[60]John Chrysostom, Homily 76, in *Commentary on Saint John the Apostle and Evangelist, Homilies 48–88*, vol. 41 of The Fathers of the Church, trans. Sr. Thomas Aquinas Goggin, S.C.H. (New York: Fathers of the Church, 1960), p. 321.

[61]Alphonsus de Liguori, *The Way to Converse Always and Familiarly with God*, pp. 400–1.

a work on patience: "Patience is the companion of wisdom."[62] Patience requires wisdom and an understanding of priorities, what is important and what is not. But patience also gives wisdom.

Saint Alphonsus points out that everyone has to suffer, but only those who have acquired wisdom find the resources to endure suffering with patience: "We must suffer, and all must suffer; be they just, or be they sinners, each one must carry his cross. He that carries it with patience is saved; he that carries it with impatience is lost."[63]

And he quotes another priest who said that being patient in suffering is a greater proof of love than offering God a great deal of praise when everything is going well: "Saint John of Avila used to say: 'One "Blessed be God" in times of adversity is worth more than a thousand acts of gratitude in times of prosperity.'"[64]

Saint Vincent de Paul was a French priest who lived in the 1600s and founded a group of mission preachers who came to be called Vincentians. He had a parable about accepting tribulation in order to grow in patience:

> There was a king who kept in prison two men owing him large sums of money. Upon seeing that they were unable to pay their debts, he threw a bag of money to each of them. Both felt the impact of the heavy bag upon their backs. One of them, angered by the blow, burst out impatiently without paying any attention to the bag. The other, paying little heed to the pain, realized the favor he had received, thanked the king, and with that money paid

---

[62] Augustine, "On Patience", 4, in vol. 3 of *Nicene and Post-Nicene Fathers*, series 1, ed. Philip Schaff (Buffalo, N.Y.: Christian Literature Publishing, 1887).

[63] Alphonsus de Liguori, *The Practice of the Love of Jesus Christ*, p. 307.

[64] Alphonsus quoting John of Avila, *Audi Filia*; cf. Alphonsus de Liguori, *Conformity to God's Will*, 2.

his debt. So it is with us. All of us owe great debts to God
for the many benefits received from him and for the many
offenses we have given him. We have no means of making
satisfaction. God, moved to pity on this account, sends us
the gold of patience in the bag of tribulations. He who
accepts his trials with patience makes satisfaction to God
with this precious gold and increases in grace. He who
does not, increases his debts and makes himself ever more
displeasing to God.[65]

The bishops of the Second Vatican Council made a special plea to the suffering:

> May all those who are weighed down with poverty, infir-
> mity and sickness, as well as those who must bear various
> hardships or who bear persecution for justice sake—may
> they all know they are united with the suffering Christ in a
> special way for the salvation of the world. The Lord called
> them blessed in His Gospel and they are those whom "the
> God of all graces, who has called us unto His eternal glory
> in Christ Jesus, will Himself, after we have suffered a little
> while, perfect, strengthen and establish" (1 Pt 5:10).[66]

Friendship makes all inconveniences bearable. Our
friendship with Christ will help us bear with patience
whatever comes into our lives. This does not mean that we
should not try to remedy bad situations, including those in
which we suffer from poor health and pain. But when we
have done all we can and trouble remains, we leave it in
God's hands and ask for the gifts of patience and peace.

Saint Francis de Sales describes the priorities of working
to improve a situation while accepting that God may have
a better idea:

[65] Vincent de Paul, quoted in *Spiritual Diary*, p. 93.
[66] Vatican II, Dogmatic Constitution on the Church, 41.

God's will is ordinarily seen in things that happen. Suppose my mother is sick in bed. How do I determine whether or not God intends for her to die? There is no way I can know this. While waiting for God's good pleasure to be revealed, I give her every remedy possible to cure her. If God gives the disease precedent over the medicines, then I will concur even though there remains a natural desire for her to live. I will pray, "Lord, her death is my will because it is your will. It has pleased you; it will please me."[67]

Forgiveness

Earlier we saw that if we want to retain our friends, we must learn to apologize and to forgive. Similarly we must be able to "forgive" God when we think we are suffering too much.

In a Jesuit high school in Saint Louis, a security guard pushed out the door the only student still in the school after hours. The guard said there was a fire in the chapel. But as the guard explained to the fire department the circumstances of discovering the fire, they noticed that his story changed significantly with each retelling. Finally, under police questioning, the security guard admitted that he had started the fire. He had gone into the chapel, he said, to say a prayer because his grandmother had recently died. But as he sat there thinking about her death, he grew angrier with God until, under the full weight of his fury, he lit the altar cloth on fire with one of the candles burning in the chapel. It was an act of revenge against God for taking his grandmother away.

It is only human to be angry with God at times. Anger is our reaction to what we perceive as injustice. To lose

---

[67] Francis de Sales, *Living Love: A Modern Edition of "Treatise on the Love of God"*, ed. Bernard Bangley (Brewster, Mass.: Paraclete Press, 2003), p. 89.

a beloved relative or to see an innocent child suffer seems so unjust to us. "Why does God let something like that happen?" we all find ourselves asking from time to time. The fact is, God, who is all goodness, love, and truth, can never be at fault. If there is any fault involved, it is that of particular individuals or of mankind in general.

There is a story about the German Lutheran theologian Dietrich Bonhoeffer, who was arrested by the Nazis for opposing their regime. During a bombing raid by the Allies, his jailer remarked to him, "How can a loving Father do this to his children?"

Bonhoeffer answered, "How can children do this to their loving Father?"

Doing the Will of God

Doing What Is Best for the Friend

In human friendships we are motivated to do what a friend requests of us. Out of love for him we gladly spend ourselves. But we have to be careful. Sometimes what a friend requests would not really be good for him. A woman told Padre Pio, the Italian mystic of the twentieth century, that she loved him more than she loved God. He told her to go into the village and steal something for him. Shocked, she refused. "You see," he said, "you do love God more than me."[68]

What God wants is always good for us. Saint Teresa of Avila writes:

In order that love be true and the friendship endure, the wills of the friends must be in accord. The will of the

[68] Cf. Dorothy Gaudiose, *Prophet of the People* (New York: Alba House, 1974), p. 32.

Lord, it is already known, cannot be at fault; our will is vicious, sensual, and ungrateful. And if you do not yet love him as he loves you because you have not reached the degree of conformity with his will, you will endure this pain of spending a long while with one who is so different from you when you see how much it benefits you to possess his friendship and how much he loves you.[69]

Saint Teresa is saying that we might not want everything that God wants because it goes so much against our fallen human nature, but if we are willing to remain friends with God, we will learn to want what he wants.

And Saint Alphonsus remarks: "And let us be persuaded that while we desire what God desires, we desire what is best for ourselves."[70]

Jesus says, "He who has my commandments and keeps them, he it is who love me; and he who loves me will be loved by my Father, and I will love him and manifest myself to him" (Jn 14:21).

Being friends with God implies trying to please him and to do what he would like. Jesus says, "You are my friends if you do what I command you" (Jn 15:14). This is why Mother Teresa of Calcutta tells us, "True holiness consists in doing God's will with a smile."[71] And Pope John Paul II says, "Holiness is the joy of doing God's will."[72]

Saint Alphonsus advises:

Manifest, then, to him freely all your state of mind, and pray to him to guide you to accomplish perfectly his holy

---

[69] Teresa of Avila, *The Book of Her Life*, 8, 5.

[70] Alphonsus de Liguori, *The Practice of the Love of Jesus Christ*, p. 405.

[71] Mother Teresa, quoted in Malcolm Muggeridge, *Something Beautiful for God* (London: Collins, 1971), p. 67.

[72] John Paul II, Homily at St. Joseph, Rome, January 18, 1981.

will. And let all your desires and plans be simply bent to discover his good pleasure, and do what is agreeable to his divine heart: "Commit your way to the LORD; trust in him and he will act" (Ps 37:5); "Bless the Lord God on every occasion; ask him that your ways be made straight and that all your paths and plans may prosper" (Tob 4:19).[73]

Saint Ambrose once said, "The will of God is the measure of all things." But how do we know God's will?

Jesus gives us two commandments: love of God and love of neighbor (Mt 22:37–40). Love of neighbor, though found in the Old Testament (see 1 Jn 3:11), is Jesus' new commandment. All will know who Jesus' disciples are by their love for one another (Jn 13:34–35).

From this notion of love we have gotten the idea that it is better to do some things because they are what God wants us to do (moral things). And we should avoid other things because God does not want us to do them (immoral things). Sin is the opposite of holiness.

The bishops of the Second Vatican Council taught:

Indeed, in order that love, as good seed may grow and bring forth fruit in the soul, each one of the faithful must willingly hear the Word of God and accept His Will, and must complete what God has begun by their own actions with the help of God's grace. These actions consist in the use of the sacraments and in a special way the Eucharist, frequent participation in the sacred action of the Liturgy, application of oneself to prayer, self-abnegation, lively fraternal service and the constant exercise of all the virtues. For charity, as the bond of perfection and the fulfillment of the law (cf. Col 3:14; Rom 13:10), rules over all

[73] Alphonsus de Liguori, *The Way to Converse Always and Familiarly with God*, p. 399.

the means of attaining holiness and gives life to these same means (cf. Rom 8:10–11). It is charity which guides us to our final end. It is the love of God and the love of one's neighbor which points out the true disciple of Christ.[74]

Those who try to do what God wants are more than his mere friends; they are like family. Jesus once remarked: " 'Who is my mother, and who are my brethren?' And stretching out his hand toward his disciples, he said, 'Here are my mother and my brethren! For whoever does the will of my Father in heaven is my brother, and sister, and mother' " (Mt 12:48–50).

Saint Bernard said that seeking God's will enables love to grow:

> The Holy Spirit lovingly visited the second power of the soul, the will. He found it infected with the poison of the body, but already judged by reason. He cleansed it with sweetness, making it burn with love and filling it with mercy, so that like a skin which is made pliable with oil it would stretch wide and bring the heavenly oil of love even to its enemies. And so from this second union, of the Spirit of God and the human will, love is born.[75]

Wisdom: Knowing God's Will

An old Teutonic myth points up the importance of wisdom:

> [Odin] was the All-father, supreme among gods and men, yet even so he constantly sought for more wisdom. He went down to the Well of Wisdom guarded by Mimir

---

[74] Vatican II, Dogmatic Constitution on the Church, 42.
[75] Bernard of Clairvaux, *On the Steps of Humility and Pride*, 7, 21.

the wise, to beg for a draught from it, and when Mimir answered that he must pay for it with one of his eyes, he consented to give the eye.[76]

But Saint Augustine warned that there is a true wisdom and a false notion of wisdom: "We are ensnared by the wisdom of the serpent; we are set free by the foolishness of God."[77]

True wisdom reveals the importance of God's commands, and the Holy Spirit of wisdom fills us with holiness: "Who has learned your counsel, unless you have given wisdom and sent your holy Spirit from on high?" (Wis 9:17). "Though she [Wisdom] is but one, she can do all things, and while remaining in herself, she renews all things; in every generation she passes into holy souls and makes them friends of God, and prophets" (Wis 7:27).

Wisdom brings friendship with God, and such wisdom is won only through self-discipline: "for it is an unfailing treasure for men; those who get it obtain friendship with God, commended for the gifts that come from instruction" (Wis 7:14). It was for their lack of loyalty and self-discipline that God at times withdrew his friendship from the ancient people of Israel: "For thus says the LORD: Do not enter the house of mourning, or go to lament, or bemoan them; for I have taken away my peace from this people, says the LORD, my steadfast love and mercy" (Jer 16:5).

Saint Paul prays for wisdom for the members of the community of Ephesus so that they can know Christ: "I do not cease to give thanks for you, remembering you in my prayers, that the God of our Lord Jesus Christ, the

---

[76] Edith Hamilton, *Mythology*, p. 308.
[77] Augustine, *On Christian Doctrine*, 1, 14, 13.

Father of glory, may give you a spirit of wisdom and of revelation in the knowledge of him" (Eph 1:16–17). He advises them to try to understand God's will: "Therefore do not be foolish, but understand what the will of the Lord is" (Eph 5:17).

Jesus said that doing the will of God is the sign that someone is a true disciple of his: "Not every one who says to me, 'Lord, Lord,' shall enter the kingdom of heaven, but he who does the will of my Father who is in heaven" (Mt 7:21).

In the garden before his death, Jesus gave an example of his own dedication to the Father's will: "And going a little farther, he fell on the ground and prayed that, if it were possible, the hour might pass from him. And he said, 'Abba, Father, all things are possible for you; remove this chalice from me; yet not what I will, but what you will'" (Mk 14:35–36).

God's will will inevitably win out. The question is whether we align ourselves with him or try to act against him. A story illustrates that truth:

Once a young novice came to his director with a question: "When people refuse to do what God wants, do they force him to change his plans?"

The director invited the novice to accompany him to where they could see the mighty river that bordered their property. "This river will inevitably flow to its destination, the sea. There is no stopping it. Knowledgeable people have respected its course and built around it. But others, in the hope of having a place for themselves, have built on the flood plain. They wanted to pretend that the river simply will not go over its banks. Do you remember the destruction of last summer?"

"Yes," said the novice. He remembered the flooding out of many homes and how he and other novices had helped clean up the mess afterward and how horrified they were to see the extent of the destruction.

"Well," continued the director, "God's will is like that mighty river, which inevitably flows on. No obstacles that human plans can put in its way will stop it. No plans that do not respect the will of God will ultimately succeed. We either cooperate with the will of God and respect it, or we oppose it to our own destruction."

Saint Alphonsus says that we mistake things that are displeasing to us as "bad": "From God come all things, good as well as evil. We call adversities evil; actually they are good and meritorious, when we receive them as coming from God's hands."[78]

Saint Clement of Rome compared the Christian's call to obedience to the kind of submission soldiers need to give their officers. "Not all are prefects, or tribunes, or centurions, or in charge of bands of fifty, and so forth; but each one in his own rank carries out the commands issued by the emperor and the officers."[79]

Finally, Saint Alphonsus tells this story about what makes a person holy:

> Cesarius points up what we have been saying by offering this incident in the life of a certain monk: Externally his religious observance was the same as that of the other monks, but he had attained such sanctity that the mere touch of his garments healed the sick. Marveling at these deeds, since his life was no more exemplary than the lives of the other monks, the superior asked him one day what was the cause of these miracles. He replied that he too was mystified and was at a loss how to account for such happenings.
>
> "What devotions do you practice?' asked the abbot.

[78] Alphonsus de Liguori, *Conformity to God's Will*, 2.
[79] Clement of Rome, *Letter to the Corinthians*, 37, 3.

He answered that there was little or nothing special that he did beyond making a great deal of willing only what God willed, and that God had given him the grace of abandoning his will totally to the will of God.

"Prosperity does not lift me up, nor adversity cast me down," added the monk. "I direct all my prayers to the end that God's will may be done fully in me and by me."

"That raid that our enemies made the other day against the monastery, in which our stores were plundered, our granaries put to the torch, and our cattle driven off—did not this misfortune cause you any resentment?" queried the abbot.

"No, Father," came the reply. "On the contrary, I returned thanks to God—as is my custom in such circumstances—fully persuaded that God does all things, or permits all that happens, for his glory and for our greater good; thus I am always at peace, no matter what happens."

Seeing such conformity with the will of God, the abbot no longer wondered why the monk worked so many miracles.[80]

The Church Teaches God's Will

Doing what is best for our friend is a sign of love. And doing what God wants is a sign of love for him. Wisdom means knowing what God wants. That kind of wisdom is a gift from God. But the Church God has given us also helps us to know what God wants.

The Church received the revelation of truth from Christ through the apostles:

Saint Jerome relates that when Saint John had reached an advanced age and was no longer able to take an active part in the sacred functions, unless supported by his disciples,

[80] Alphonsus de Liguori, *Conformity to God's Will*, 2.

or to give long sermons due to his weakened voice, he would repeatedly urge, "Little children, love one another." Weary of the same few words, his hearers asked him why he always preached thus to them. "Because," he answered, "this is the Lord's precept, and if you observe it, that alone is enough."[81]

The *Catechism* emphasizes the same point: "The entire Law of the Gospel is contained in the '*new commandment*' of Jesus, to love one another as he has loved us" (1970).[82]

The Church offers a number of helps to a person who wishes to live according to God's will. The *Catechism* tells us:

> It is in the Church, in communion with all the baptized, that the Christian fulfills his vocation. From the Church he receives the Word of God containing the teachings of "the law of Christ."[83] From the Church he receives the grace of the sacraments that sustains him on the "way." From the Church he learns the *example of holiness* and recognizes its model and source in the all-holy Virgin Mary; he discerns it in the authentic witness of those who live it; he discovers it in the spiritual tradition and long history of the saints who have gone before him and whom the liturgy celebrates in the rhythms of the sanctoral cycle. (2030)

Those who have the responsibility of teaching in the Church come to realize that it is more by what they do than by what they say that the faithful understand the law of love:

> When he became a bishop, Venerable de Palafox gave a dinner every Thursday to twelve poor people. He himself waited on them. Then, in reading the life of Saint Martin,

---

[81] *Spiritual Diary*, p. 233.
[82] Cf. Jn 15:12; 13:34.
[83] Gal 6:2.

he found that this saint not only served the poor but even washed their feet. The holy bishop decided to do likewise. He performed all these services with as much satisfaction and attention as if he had been waiting on Jesus Christ himself. This produced in him a great respect for the poor, and each time he met a needy person he seemed to see God himself.[84]

And the faithful come to learn that obedience to the bishops and their representatives is a form of love. When Saint Monica was told that the bishop Saint Ambrose had forbidden people from making a tour of the memorial shrines to the martyrs, and from sharing meals including wine there, she stopped what had been her custom. Augustine remarks: "When she learned that the bishop had forbidden this, she accepted it so reverently and obediently that I myself was amazed at how easily she became an incriminator of her own custom, rather than an adjudicator of this prohibition."[85]

Even saints at times found it challenging to give their loyal obedience to what a bishop or a pope asked of them. Take Saint Alphonsus, for instance. On July 21, 1773, pressured by several kings and political leaders, for purely political reasons, Pope Clement XIV issued a letter suppressing the Society of Jesus. When Alphonsus heard the news, he was thunderstruck—literally speechless. Eventually, he had the opportunity to read the letter. He simply said, "The pope's will, God's will," and made no further reference to the incident, but his depression, evident in his face, continued for some time.[86]

Alphonsus' example had its effect on a later pope, John XXIII, who wrote this journal entry as a young priest:

---

[84] *Spiritual Diary*, p. 236.
[85] Augustine, *Confessions*, 6, 2.
[86] Cf. John XXIII, *Journal of a Soul*, p. 177, n. 3.

I confirm my last year's intention about guarding my loyalty of heart and mind to the Church and the Pope. In
days of uncertainty and sadness Saint Alphonsus used to say:
"The Pope's will: God's will!" This shall be my motto and I
will be true to it. O Lord, help me, for I desire you alone![87]

The Church, through the revelation that Christ has
entrusted to her, guides us in a general way in doing the
will of God. It is necessary in particular situations, however, to pray and to consult others who are wise and well
practiced in the things of God. There are no shortcuts to
discerning the will of God, as the following joke illustrates:

Sister Superior needed some guidance in making a decision, so she consulted the Bible. She opened a page at
random, placed her finger blindly in the book, and then
read the passage: "Judas went out and hanged himself." A
bit flustered by this, she decided to try again. This time her
finger indicated the passage "Go and do likewise." Now,
really intent upon clearing up the gathering confusion,
she decided to try once more. Her finger pointed to the
phrase: "What you do, do quickly."

In considering a particular course of action in our lives,
instead of asking ourselves, "What do I want to do?" we
should rather ask ourselves, "What does God want me
to do?"

In the area of moral theology the Church has the authority to teach us: we should not commit adultery, murder,
theft, et cetera. We should aid the poor and be responsible
for our families, to society, and to those who exercise just
authority.

But in other areas the Church can be of help to us in
only a very broad way: Should I go to college? Should
I move to another house? Whom should I marry? What

---

[87] Written during a retreat when he was thirty years old. Ibid. p. 177.

career should I follow? Do I have a call to the priesthood or the religious life?

In our prayer, we should ask the Lord to clarify for us what he wants. Surely God will help us to know what he wants us to do, but we need to show we are interested.

We should consult people who have Christ at the center of their lives. Saint Alphonsus used to consult several learned and holy people before making any important decision. The Scriptures say: "Where there is no guidance, a people falls; but in an abundance of counselors there is safety" (Prov 11:14).

After getting the advice of others and while continuing to pray for God's guidance, we should weigh the factors, pro and con, and pay attention to our inner stirrings. And then we should make a decision.

Not to make a decision or not to act is itself a decision. Abba Ammonas, one of the Fathers of the Desert, said:

> Imagine discernment as an axe. Some are content with thinking of themselves as possessing it, but since they never use it, they spend their whole lives without ever cutting down a single tree. Others are experienced at wielding an axe. With just a few blows they can fell a tree.[88]

Fraternal Correction

True friends are able to give and accept correction. If we are afraid that someone will take exception to a word of advice or correction from us, we would have to wonder about the strength of the friendship. How does this apply to our friendship with God?

---

[88] Abba Ammonas, quoted in *The Sayings of the Desert Fathers*, trans. Benedicta Ward (London: Mowbrays, 1975), p. 174.

Giving Correction

In our saner moments we realize that it would be arrogant beyond belief to want to correct the Lord. He who is all good and all just and is truth and love itself does not need our correction any more than a famous artist would seek the counsel of a toddler in his painting.

But on the level of the feelings, we may become irritated or at least confused by the direction things take in our lives, and we may wonder what the Lord means by it all. There is a famous story about Saint Teresa of Avila, who was riding in a horse-drawn wagon on her way to the village one day. The wagon tipped and threw her into the mud. She got up, brushed herself off as best she could, and was heard to mutter to the Lord, "If this is the way you treat your friends, it is no wonder you have so few of them!"

Rather than finding ourselves wanting to give correction to the Lord, it is more likely that we would have to give correction to others.

One of the most beautiful signs that a married couple has bonded is their solicitude for one another. The wife will not let her husband out of the house until his hair is neatly combed, there are no buttons missing from his suit, and nothing about his appearance will reflect badly on him. Similarly, a husband is deeply offended when his wife is insulted. If the spouses do these things for each other out of affection for each other, the care they show each other strengthens the bond of their love.

There is also a lesson to be learned about what our desire should be to defend the honor of God and the name of Jesus. There is a story about a rabbi who was hailed before the Roman emperor. "Let me see this God of yours," the emperor demanded.

"Then look up to the sky," said the rabbi.

When the emperor did so, he looked at the sun and was momentarily blinded. He had to put his hand before his eyes.

"What?" exclaimed the rabbi. "You want to see the Master when you can't even bear to see the servant?"[89]

But in correcting others in their mistreatment of the Lord and in their misunderstanding of him, we need to be careful not to descend into self-righteousness. Abba Macarius, one of the Fathers of the Desert, said, "If you reprove someone, you yourself get carried away by anger and you are satisfying your own passion; do not lose yourself, therefore, in order to save another."[90]

Accepting Correction

The Scriptures point out that the Lord corrects us at times, and it is a blessing: "My son, do not despise the LORD's discipline or be weary of his reproof, for the LORD reproves him whom he loves, as a father the son in whom he delights" (Prov 3:11–12).

Saint Clement of Alexandria compared loving correction to good medicine:

Reproof is like surgery performed on the passions of the soul; the passions are like a disease of truth, which need to be removed by the surgeon's knife. Rebuke is like a physic, dissolving the hardness of passion and purging the lusts, the impurities of life; besides, it levels the swelling of pride and restores man to normalcy and health. Then there is admonition, which is like the diet given one who

[89] Cf. F.H. Drinkwater, *Catechism Stories* (Westminster, Md.: Newman Press, 1948), p. 20.

[90] Abba Macarius, quoted in *The Sayings of the Desert Fathers*, p. 131.

is sick, counseling what should be taken and forbidding what should not. All these things tend to salvation and eternal good health.[91]

Each of us should accept in our lives the warnings that our weaknesses give us. Using a medical metaphor as well, Saint Bernard describes temptation as a necessary corrective to special consolations, such as revelations:

> For the physician uses not only ointments but fire and iron, with which he cuts and burns away whatever is superfluous and brings healing by the wound he causes. He removes anything which would prevent the ointment from healing. In the same way, God, the physician of souls, brings temptations upon the soul and sends tribulations. And when it is afflicted and humiliated by these, its joy turns to sorrow (Bar 4:34; Jas 4:9). It thinks what has been revealed to it is an illusion. So it comes to be free of vanity, and the truth of the revelation endures.[92]

Through his Church God offers direction and even correction to people whose lives would otherwise end in personal disaster. Pope Saint Gregory recommended that pastors be not afraid to correct members of their flock: "The word of reproach is a key that unlocks a door, because reproach reveals a fault of which the evildoer is himself often unaware."[93]

Eutropius had been imperial minister when Saint John Chrysostom was made archbishop of Constantinople. The two became enemies when Chrysostom began denouncing the injustices of the rich. Soon, however, Eutropius

---

[91] Clement of Alexandria, *Christ the Educator*, 1, 8, 64–65.

[92] Bernard of Clairvaux, *On the Steps of Humility and Pride*, 10, 37.

[93] Gregory the Great, *The Book of Pastoral Rule*, in vol. 12 of *Nicene and Post-Nicene Fathers*, 2nd series, trans. Rev. James Barmby, D.D., eds. Philip Schaff and Henry Wace (Buffalo, N.Y.: Christian Literature Publishing, 1895).

himself was sought as an enemy of the emperor. He fled to the cathedral for refuge and stood there, clinging to the altar for his life, when Chrysostom ascended the pulpit to preach. Chrysostom's sermon was directed, in part, to the quaking Eutropius:

> Did I not always tell you that riches are fleeting, a thank-less servant? But you would not listen to me. And now you know that they are murderous as well, for they are the cause of your fear and trembling. When you rebuked me for telling you the truth, did I not say, "I love you better than do your flatterers; I, who reprove you, care more for you than do your obsequious friends"? ... Your false friends have deserted you, seeking their own safety: it is otherwise with us. The Church, whom you treated as an enemy, has opened her arms and taken you to her heart: but the theater and circus, which you angrily defended against my attacks, have betrayed you.[94]

Asking God for Forgiveness

Once we recognize that we can make mistakes and once we have the humility to own up to them, we should also ask pardon of God.

We seriously misunderstand God if we think that he is a policeman who delights in catching us at our sins: "Say to them, As I live, says the Lord GOD, I have no pleasure in the death of the wicked, but that the wicked turn from his way and live" (Ezek 33:11).

Saint Alphonsus had this to say about repentance:

> Attend greatly, devout soul, to the instruction commonly given by masters of the spiritual life: after your unfaithful

[94]John Chrysostom, "On the Fall of Eutropius", in Donald Attwater, *St. John Chrysostom: The Voice of Gold* (Milwaukee: Bruce, 1939), pp. 96–97.

conduct, at once to have recourse to God, though you have repeated it a hundred times in a day; and after your falls, and the recourse you have had to the Lord (as has just been said), at once to be in peace. Otherwise, while you remain cast down and disturbed at the fault you have committed, your converse with God will be small; your trust in him will fail; your desire to love him [will] grow cold; and you will be little able to go forward in the way of the Lord. On the other hand, by having immediate recourse to God to ask his forgiveness, and to promise him amendment, your very faults will serve to advance you further in the divine love. Between friends who sincerely love each other it often happens that when one has displeased the other, and then humbles himself and asks pardon, their friendship thereby becomes stronger than ever. Do you likewise; see to it that your very faults serve to bind you yet closer in love to your God.[95]

Saint Francis de Sales also urged gentleness with ourselves in our sins:

Believe me, Philothea, a father's gentle, loving rebuke has far greater power to correct a child than rage and passion. So too when we have committed some fault, if we rebuke our heart by a calm, mild remonstrance, with more compassion for it than passion against it and encourage it to make amendment, then repentance conceived in this way will sink far deeper and penetrate more effectually than fretful, angry, stormy repentance.[96]

Fr. Mark Link, S.J., tells what he calls a medieval story about the value of repentance:

A woman who had not lived an altogether good life died. Saint Peter refused to let her into heaven until she

---

[95] Alphonsus de Liguori, *The Way to Converse Always and Familiarly with God*, pp. 405–6.

[96] Francis de Sales, *Introduction to the Devout Life*, 3, 9.

brought with her "what God values most". She was not sure what it was that God values most.

She returned to earth and found that a martyr had died. She brought a drop of his blood with her but still was not admitted into heaven.

She returned to earth again and found a missionary who had labored all his life in proclaiming the Word of God. She brought back to heaven a drop of sweat from his brow but still was not admitted into heaven.

She was confused as to what God would value the most. But then she saw a little child with a most innocent countenance standing by a pond. At the same time, she saw a man on horseback ride up; he also saw the child's innocence. The rider caught a glimpse of his own face in the pond and began to cry for the innocence he had lost. The woman brought to heaven a teardrop from the repentant sinner and was admitted to heaven amid great rejoicing from the angels and saints. For she had found "what God values most": the tears of the repentant.

Jesus himself said the same thing when he was criticized for accepting the tearful homage of a woman, whom some have thought was Mary Magdalene, who was known in the town for her dissolute life: "Therefore I tell you, her sins, which are many, are forgiven, for she loved much; but he who is forgiven little, loves little" (Lk 7:47).

Saint Thérèse of Lisieux loved much even though she had no need to be forgiven much. But she was wise enough to see the hand of God giving her that freedom to avoid sin:

> I find such comfort in those penetrating words of our Lord to Simon the Pharisee: "He loves little, who has little forgiven him" (Lk 7:47). But I, you say, owed him little? On the contrary, I owe him more than the Magdalene

herself; he remitted my sins beforehand, as it were, by not letting me fall into them. Oh dear, I wish I could explain exactly what I feel about it. Put it like this—a clever doctor has a son who trips over a stone, falls, and breaks a limb. His father is at his side in a moment, picks him up tenderly, and treats his injuries with all the skill he has. Thanks to him, the boy is completely cured before long; and the father, sure enough, has done something to earn his love. But now, suppose the father sees the stone in his son's path, runs ahead of him and takes it out of the way, without calling any attention to what he is doing. At the time, the boy is unconscious of the danger he would have run, but for his father's foresight; [he] is less grateful, less moved to affection, than if a cure had been performed. But if he learns afterward what risks he has been spared, the boy will love him more than ever. And that's what God's loving providence has done for me. When he sent his Son into the world, it was to ransom sinners, not the just—yes, but, you see, in my case he has left me in debt to him not for much but for everything. He hasn't waited to make me love him much, like the Magdalene; he's made me realize what I owe to his tender foresight, to make me love him to distraction, as I do. When I'm told that an innocent soul can't love as a repentant soul does, how I long to give that sentiment the lie![97]

The Ability to Choose to Love God or to Sin

The book of Genesis tells us that man was made in the image of God. The way in which we alone of all earthly creatures resemble God is in our ability to know and love. Only man can make a free choice to honor or love another. These are godlike capabilities.

[97] Thérèse of Lisieux, *Autobiography of St. Thérèse of Lisieux*, pp. 113–14.

How often have we told someone who has done some nice thing for us, "You didn't have to do that"? And that was exactly the point: by doing us a favor when he did not have to, he showed us that we were special and beloved to him.

Similarly, to choose to do God's will is the same as loving God: "It was he who created man in the beginning, and he left him in the power of his own inclination. If you will, you can keep the commandments, they will save you" (Sir 15:14–15).

Saint Augustine also noted the connection between goodness and freedom: "The good man, although he is a slave, is free; but the bad man, even if he reigns, is a slave."[98] The *Catechism* observes: "The more one does what is good, the freer one becomes" (1733). Thomas Merton puts it this way: "Freedom ... [consists] in the perfect love and acceptance of what is really good."[99]

A little word study shows the link between "love" and "freedom" in the English language: the contemporary English word "free" comes from the Old English word *freo*. Both are related to the German word *frei*. They have their base in the Sanskrit word *priya*, meaning "agreeable" or "beloved". In ancient times, wealthier households consisted of two groups: the beloved family members, who were free, and the household slaves. If the head of the household particularly cherished a certain slave, he might "free" him. So the English word "free" refers to someone who is not a slave. And the person loving the free person was *freond*, which grew to be "friend".[100]

---

[98] Augustine, *City of God*, 4, 3.

[99] Thomas Merton, *New Seeds of Contemplation* (Norfolk, Conn.: New Directions, 1962), p. 199.

[100] See Wilfred Funk, *Word Origins and Their Romantic Stories* (New York: Wilfred Funk, 1950), p. 60.

In the concentration camps of Nazi Germany, Viktor Frankl, a Jewish psychiatrist, saw examples of the kind of person who is free because of his goodness and love. Frankl said there were some who, in spite of their own sufferings, would console others and give them some of the little food they themselves had. Such people, he said, were truly free.

As a Greek proverb puts it, "No one is free who is not master of himself." When we are at the whim of our desires, we are not free: "Liberty does not dwell in a heart subject to desires, for that heart is in captivity, but in that which is free, the heart of a son", says Saint John of the Cross.[101] By focusing on pleasing the Lord rather than ourselves, we become truly free: "Who is the man that fears the LORD? Him will he instruct in the way he should choose" (Ps 25:12).

According to Saint Gregory of Nyssa, when we make the right choices in life, in a sense we bring ourselves to birth: "We are in a sense our own parents, and we give birth to ourselves by our own free choice of what is good. Such a choice becomes possible for us when we have received God into ourselves and have become children of God, children of the Most High."[102]

Ancient wisdom simplifies the choice of evil or good as being the choice between two ultimates: "There are two paths: one leads to life and one leads to death."[103]

Thomas Merton, in his autobiography, *The Seven Storey Mountain*,[104] tells of how one night, when he was a

---

[101] John of the Cross, *The Ascent of Mount Carmel*, 1, 4, 6.

[102] Gregory of Nyssa in a homily on Ecclesiastes, in *The Liturgy of the Hours*, 3:238.

[103] *Didache*, 1, 1.

[104] Thomas Merton, *The Seven Storey Mountain* (San Diego: Harcourt, Brace, Jovanovich, 1976), pp. 40–41.

boy living in a small town in France, he and several other passengers were in a car being driven by a local young man. The young driver caught sight of a rabbit running in the road and sped up in an attempt to kill the rabbit. The rabbit zigzagged back and forth across the road, staying some five feet ahead of the car, its white tail bobbing in the headlights. The passengers became more and more nervous as the car careened along. They protested, but the young driver was intent on killing the rabbit. They came over the top of a hill and sped down it. The protests grew louder because the passengers were afraid the car would turn over and tumble down a long incline into the river below. The young man carried on his relentless pursuit, the rabbit successfully dodging his every move. Finally, all the passengers together called out that they were approaching a wall. The road forked off in two directions from that dead end. Just in time, the driver swerved down one of the forks and put on the brakes.

"Did you catch him?" asked Merton.

"Oh, no," replied the driver sadly, "he took the other road."

I no longer remember what point Merton was making with the story, but it certainly can illustrate how elusive is the choice to make some earthbound pleasure our ultimate happiness.

People who make a choice in favor of some temporary satisfaction (wealth, pleasure, fame, et cetera) over eternal life are like the prisoner who chooses the company of the jailer over the pardon of the governor.

Once two young sisters left home to find work in a city far away. Soon after they had rented an apartment and found jobs, they received a letter from an uncle. He had won the lottery and now was inviting them to return home, where he promised he would take good care of them. He enclosed money for their plane flight.

At the travel agency, one of the sisters noticed posters advertising vacation cruises to faraway places.

"Look, Brenda," Alice said, "This cruise costs the very same amount that Uncle sent us. Why don't we go on the cruise and have fun?"

"But Uncle sent us that money so that we could get back home," Brenda cautioned. "He said he would take care of us once we got there and we would not have to worry about money."

A heated argument ensued, and as a result, each girl went her own way. Brenda took the flight back home. Alice took the vacation cruise.

Alice enjoyed the cruise immensely, but afterward she had to find another job and an affordable apartment to be able to survive.

Meanwhile, Brenda returned to her hometown. Her uncle had a home built for her and set up a trust fund for her, and not long afterward she married her hometown sweetheart.

Choices that we make for short-term enjoyment may rob us of long-term happiness.[105]

Jesus says, "Enter by the narrow gate; for the gate is wide and the way is easy, that leads to destruction, and those who enter by it are many. For the gate is narrow and the way is hard, that leads to life, and those who find it are few" (Mt 7:13–14). And Saint John tells us: "By this it may be seen who are the children of God, and who are the children of the devil: whoever does not do right is not of God, nor he who does not love his brother" (1 Jn 3:10).

---

[105] Based on F. H. Drinkwater, *Catechism Stories*, pp. 6–7.

The Sacrament of Reconciliation

Sin is a reality in our lives. And so is the forgiveness of God.

In the Old Testament, we are constantly reminded of God's readiness to forgive: "For your name's sake, O LORD, pardon my guilt, for it is great" (Ps 25:11). "[T]hough your sins are like scarlet, they shall be as white as snow; though they are red like crimson, they shall become like wool" (Is 1:18).

In the New Testament, Jesus shows the forgiveness of God: "And behold, they brought to him a paralytic, lying on his bed; and when Jesus saw their faith, he said to the paralytic, 'Take heart, my son; your sins are forgiven'" (Mt 9:2).

Jesus says the person who is forgiven more will love more:

> "A certain creditor had two debtors; one owed five hundred denarii, and the other fifty. When they could not pay, he forgave them both. Now which of them will love him more?" Simon answered, "The one, I suppose, to whom he forgave more." And he said to him, "You have judged rightly." (Lk 7:41–43)

In the Catholic Church, the usual forum for asking and receiving God's forgiveness is in the sacrament of Reconciliation or Penance, or Confession. According to the *Roman Catechism*, which was drawn up after the Council of Trent: "The whole power of the sacrament of Penance consists in restoring us to God's grace and joining us with him in an intimate friendship."[106]

---

[106] *Roman Catechism*, 2, 5, 18, quoted in the *Catechism of the Catholic Church* (1468).

The *Catechism of the Catholic Church* explains:

Over the centuries the concrete form in which the Church has exercised this power received from the Lord has varied considerably. During the first centuries the reconciliation of Christians who had committed particularly grave sins after their Baptism (for example, idolatry, murder, or adultery) was tied to a very rigorous discipline, according to which penitents had to do public penance for their sins, often for years, before receiving reconciliation. To this "order of penitents" (which concerned only certain grave sins), one was only rarely admitted and in certain regions only once in a lifetime. During the seventh century Irish missionaries, inspired by the Eastern monastic tradition, took to continental Europe the "private" practice of penance, which does not require public and prolonged completion of penitential works before reconciliation with the Church. From that time on, the sacrament has been performed in secret between penitent and priest. This new practice envisioned the possibility of repetition and so opened the way to a regular frequenting of this sacrament. It allowed the forgiveness of grave sins and venial sins to be integrated into one sacramental celebration. In its main lines this is the form of penance that the Church has practiced down to our day. (1447)

The *Catechism* goes on to say: "Because sin is always an offense against God, only he can forgive it" (431).[107] But the forgiveness comes through the instrumentality of a priest: his words, his kindness, sometimes his reassuring embrace. After his Resurrection, Jesus appeared to his apostles:

Jesus said to them again, "Peace be with you. As the Father has sent me, even so I send you." And when he had said

[107] Cf. Ps 51:4, 12.

this, he breathed on them, and said to them, "Receive the Holy Spirit. If you forgive the sins of any, they are forgiven; if you retain the sins of any, they are retained" (Jn 20:21–23).

We have a psychological need to hear that we are forgiven, not just in general terms—for our part in the sins of all mankind in general—but particularly for some specific sin at some specific time. Once I was called to the hospital on a Sunday morning between Masses. A young man wanted to go to Confession. I invited him to begin, and he said that he did not know how. It turned out that he was not Catholic. I asked why he would want to go to Confession if he was not Catholic. He said he had done some things wrong and did not know where else to turn to confess them.

We know without a doubt when we have done something truly terribly wrong, a mortal sin, which has left us feeling dead inside. We will not feel relief until we have been able to confess it and hear, from the representative of God himself, that we have been forgiven.

Frequent confession—every month or six weeks—is also a good way to keep our predominant fault in check. The *Catechism* advises:

> Without being strictly necessary, confession of everyday faults (venial sins) is nevertheless strongly recommended by the Church.[108] Indeed the regular confession of our venial sins helps us form our conscience, fight against evil tendencies, let ourselves be healed by Christ and progress in the life of the Spirit (1458).

The net result of the experience of pardon is gratitude and love. Saint Bernard says:

[108] Cf. Council of Trent: DS 1680; CIC, can. 988 § 2.

Take away condemnation, take away fear, take away confusion, and there is full remission of sins. Then our sins
will not be against us but will work together for good
(Rom 8:28), so that we may give devout thanks to him
who has remitted them.[109]

"Blessed is he whose transgression is forgiven, whose sin
is covered" (Ps 32:1).

Love: The Antidote for Sin

Love is a powerful antidote to the troubles we encoun-
ter, and cause, in life: "Above all hold unfailing your love
for one another, since love covers a multitude of sins"
(1 Pet 4:8).

In Russian writer Fyodor Dostoyevsky's short story "A
Strange Man's Dream", a man contemplates suicide and
places a loaded revolver on the table next to him. But
while he awaits the right moment to pull the trigger, he
falls asleep and has a strange dream. In the dream, he has
already committed suicide. Some loathsome being leads
him by the hand into the farthest reaches of the universe,
where he alights on an earthlike planet, where the people
are as yet unspoiled by sin. He comes to know them and
at one point introduces sin to them. "It was just a little
fib," he says. Deception leads to passion, passion to jealousy, jealousy to quarreling, quarreling to violence. And
before long he has corrupted completely the people of
this paradise.

If the process of sin is gradual, the healing process of
love also rebuilds gradually. The introduction of love into
a situation tends to inspire further acts of love and healing

---

[109] Bernard of Clairvaux, *On Conversion*, 15, 28.

in others. Direct confrontation of sin is not always the best answer for its removal. Principally, living a life of good example says more than demands or threats.

A theologian approached Saint Francis of Assisi one day and wanted him to explain this passage from the book of Ezekiel: "If I say to the wicked, 'You shall surely die,' and you give him no warning, nor speak to warn the wicked from his wicked way, in order to save his life, that wicked man shall die in his iniquity; but his blood I will require at your hand." Francis protested that he was a fool and would not know about such things. The theologian persisted, "Does not the passage mean that unless you warn the wicked, all kinds of wickedness will come upon you?"

"No," answered Francis. "I take the sense to be this: The servant of God should so burn with holiness that he becomes an example to others. His splendor and the perfume of his name should be enough to warn the wicked of their iniquities."[110]

We begin our campaign of love by being sure to forgive those who have offended us: "Forgive your neighbor the wrong he has done, and then your sins will be pardoned when you pray" (Sir 28:2). Jesus said, "For if you forgive men their trespasses, your heavenly Father also will forgive you; but if you do not forgive men their trespasses, neither will your Father forgive your trespasses" (Mt 6:14–15). Forgiveness will be followed by service, fellowship, and self-sacrifice: all the things that go into making men friends with one another.

[110]Payne, *The Fathers of the Western Church*, pp. 267–68.

CONCLUSION

A thought has haunted me throughout this whole consideration of holiness and how it is related to friendship: Are there people who simply are not capable of being loved by others? How could they ever become practiced enough in the ways of friendship to find friendship with the Lord?

I think that there are no such persons who are condemned to remain friendless. First of all, of course, the Lord himself loves each of us with supreme love. He would not have given his life for someone he does not love.

But in addition to being loved by God, we are all able to be loved by others. We invite that love, however, by loving others first. As we resemble the Lord more and more in our love for others, they are drawn to us. What we look like and what natural gifts we possess have very little bearing then. The advice of Saint John of the Cross comes to the fore: "Where there is no love put love and you shall find love."[1]

A father called his three sons to him and said he would share with them a glass of wine. When they arrived, each had brought his own receptacle for the wine. The first son brought a saucer. It could not contain much and spilled easily. The second son had a dirty cup, and the

---

[1]John of the Cross, Letter 26 to Madre Maria de la Encarnacion, Segovia, July 6, 1591, in *The Collected Works of John of the Cross*, rev. ed., trans. Kieran Kavanaugh, O.C.D., and Otilio Rodriquez, O.C.D. (Washington, D.C.: ICS Publications, 1991), p. 760.

father would not entrust his precious wine to him in so dirty a container. The third son brought a wineglass. It was sturdy and clean and could receive the whole gift of the father.

Our obligation is not to be successful in being accepted as a friend by others. Our obligation is to do as the Lord himself does: to receive the love of the Father and to offer our love to others. We give the wine of friendship, and just as heartily we must be prepared to receive it from others. If others will not offer it to us, or if others will not receive it from us, it is not our responsibility. Ours is only to give good wine and to receive it in a pure vessel.

Saint Paul says:

> Love is patient and kind; love is not jealous or boastful; it is not arrogant or rude. Love does not insist on its own way; it is not irritable or resentful; it does not rejoice at wrong, but rejoices in the right. Love bears all things, believes all things, hopes all things, endures all things. Love never ends. (1 Cor 13:4–8)

His description of love is a recipe for being a friend to others, and thus for having friends.

Finally, Saint Aelred, who cherished friendship, both with other people and with Christ, was perhaps thinking of Paul's description of love when he said:

> Turn your attention briefly to the manner in which friend-ship is, so to say, a stage toward the love and knowledge of God. Indeed, in friendship there is nothing dishonor-able, nothing deceptive, nothing feigned, whatever there is, is holy, voluntary, and true.... In friendship are joined honor and charm, truth and joy, sweetness and goodwill, affection and action. And all these take their beginning

from Christ, advance through Christ, and are perfected in Christ. Therefore, not too steep or unnatural does the ascent appear from Christ, as the inspiration of the love by which we love our friend, to Christ giving himself to us as our Friend for us to love.[2]

[2] Aelred of Rievaulx, *Spiritual Friendship*, 2, 20.

ACKNOWLEDGMENTS

With grateful acknowledgment for the permission to use excerpts from the following publications:

The Art of Loving, by Erich Fromm. © 1956 by Harper and Row, New York.

The Collected Works of Saint Teresa of Avila, vol. 1. Translated by Kieran Kavanaugh and Otilio Rodriguez. © 1976 by the Washington Province of Discalced Carmelites, ICS Publications, Washington, D.C.

Introduction to the Devout Life, by Saint Francis de Sales. Translated and edited by John K. Ryan. Published 1989 by Doubleday, New York. Permission granted by the Estate of Rev. Msgr. John Ryan and the Society for the Propagation of the Faith, New York.

Living Love: A Modern Edition of "Treatise on the Love of God", by Saint Francis de Sales. Edited by Bernard Bangley. © 2003 by Bernard Bangley. Used with permission of Paraclete Press, Orleans, Massachusetts.

Mythology, by Edith Hamilton. © 1969 by Little, Brown and Company, Boston.

Spiritual Diary: Selected Sayings and Examples of the Saints. © 1962 by St. Paul Editions, Boston.

BIBLIOGRAPHY

Aelred of Rievaulx. *Aelred of Rievaulx: The Way of Friendship*. Edited by Basil M. Pennington. Hyde Park, N.Y.: New City Press, 2001.

The Apostolic Fathers. Translated by Francis X. Glimm; Joseph M.-F. Marique, S.J.; and Gerald G. Walsh, S.J. In *The Fathers of the Church*. New York: Christian Heritage, 1947.

Aquinas, Thomas. *Summa Theologica*. Vols. 1–3. New York: Benziger Brothers, 1947, 1948.

Aristotle. *The Nicomachean Ethics*. Translated by Martin Ostwald. Indianapolis: Bobbs-Merrill, 1978.

Athanasius. *Against the Heathens*. Edited by Alexander Roberts and James Donaldson. In *Nicene and Post-Nicene Fathers*, second series, vol. 4. Buffalo, N.Y.: Christian Literature Publishing, 1885.

Attwater, Donald. *St. John Chrysostom: The Voice of Gold*. Milwaukee: Bruce, 1939.

Augustine. *Christian Instruction*. Translated by John J. Gavigan, O.S.A. In *Writings of Saint Augustine*. The Fathers of the Church, vol. 4. Washington, D.C.: Catholic University of America Press, 1947.

———. *The City of God*. Translated by Marcus Dods, D.D. New York: Modern Library, 1950.

———. *Confessions*. Translated by Vernon J. Bourke, Ph.D. Washington, D.C.: Catholic University of America Press, 1953.

———. *Homilies on the Gospel of John*. Edited by Alexander Roberts and James Donaldson. In *Nicene and*

Post-Nicene Fathers, first series, vol. 7. Grand Rapids, Mich.: Eerdmans, 1950.

————. *Letters of Saint Augustine*. Selected and edited by John Leinenweber. Tarrytown, N.Y.: Triumph Books, 1992.

————. *On Christian Doctrine*. Translated by Rev. Marcus Dods, D.D. In *The Works of Aurelius Augustine*, vol. 9. Edinburgh: T&T Clark, 1873.

————. *On Faith in Things Unseen*. Translated by Roy Joseph Deferrari and Mary Francis McDonald, O.P. In *Writings of Saint Augustine*. The Fathers of the Church, vol. 4. New York: Fathers of the Church, 1947.

————. *Sermons on the Liturgical Seasons*. Translated by Sr. Mary Sarah Muldowney, R.S.M. The Fathers of the Church, vol. 38. New York: Fathers of the Church, 1959.

Bernard of Clairvaux. *On the Steps of Humility and Pride*. In *Bernard of Clairvaux: Selected Writings*. Edited by G. R. Evans. Classics of Western Spirituality, vol. 56. New York: Paulist Press, 1987.

Bernardin, Joseph. *The Gift of Peace*. New York: Image Books, 1998.

Bishop, Jim. *The Day Christ Died*. New York: Harper, 1957.

Bosco, John. *The Life of Saint Dominic Savio*. Translated by P. Aronica. New Rochelle, N.Y.: 1955.

Butler's Lives of the Saints. 4 vols. Edited, revised, and supplemented by Herbert Thurston, S.J., and Donald Attwater. New York: P. J. Kenedy and Sons, 1956.

Carnegie, Dale. *How to Win Friends and Influence People*. New York: Simon and Schuster, 1937.

Carr, John. *To Heaven through a Window: Saint Gerard Majella*. New York: Declan X. McMullen, 1949.

Castle, Tony. *More Quotes and Anecdotes*. Northport, N.Y.: Costello Publishing, 1986.

Catechism of the Catholic Church. 2nd ed. Rome: Libreria Editrice Vaticana, 1997.

Chrysologus, Peter. *Saint Peter Chrysologus: Selected Sermons and Saint Valerian: Homilies*. Translated by George E. Ganss., S.J. The Fathers of the Church, vol. 17. New York: Fathers of the Church, 1953.

Chrysostom, John. *Baptismal Instructions*, no. 1. Translated and annotated by Paul W. Harkins, Ph.D., L.L.D. Ancient Christian Writers, no. 31. New York: Paulist Press, 1963.

———. *Commentary on Saint John the Apostle and Evangelist, Homilies 1–47*. Translated by Sr. Thomas Aquinas Goggin, S.C.H. The Fathers of the Church, vol. 33. Washington, D.C.: Catholic University of America Press, 1957.

———. *Commentary on Saint John the Apostle and Evangelist, Homilies 48–88*. Translated by Sr. Thomas Aquinas Goggin, S.C.H. The Fathers of the Church, vol. 41. New York: Fathers of the Church, 1960.

———. *Homilies on Hebrews*. Translated by Frederic Gardiner. Edited by Philip Schaff. *Nicene and Post-Nicene Fathers*, first series, vol. 14. Buffalo, N.Y.: Christian Literature Publishing, 1889.

Clement of Alexandria. *Clement of Alexandria: Christ the Educator*. Translated by Simon P. Wood, C.P. The Fathers of the Church, vol. 23. New York: Fathers of the Church, 1954.

Cristiani, Leon. *St. Bernard of Clairvaux*. Boston: St. Paul Editions, 1983.

Cyril of Jerusalem. *The Works of Saint Cyril of Jerusalem*. Translated by Leo P. McCauley, S.J., and Anthony A. Stephenson. The Fathers of the Church, vols. 1

and 2. Washington, D.C.: Catholic University of America Press, 1969, 1970.

Dale, Alzina Stone. *The Outline of Sanity*. Grand Rapids, Mich.: Eerdmans, 1982.

De Sales, Francis. *Introduction to the Devout Life*. Translated and edited by John K. Ryan. New York: Image Books, 1989.

————. *Living Love: A Modern Edition of "Treatise on the Love of God"*. Edited by Bernard Bangley. Brewster, Mass.: Paraclete Press, 2003.

Donald, David Herbert. *Lincoln*. New York: Simon and Schuster, 1995.

Drinkwater, F. H. *Catechism Stories*. Westminster, Md.: Newman Press, 1948.

Fromm, Erich. *The Art of Loving*. New York: Harper, 1956.

Funk, Wilfred. *Word Origins and Their Romantic Stories*. New York: Wilfred Funk, 1950.

Gaudiose, Dorothy. *Prophet of the People*. New York: Alba House, 1974.

Gregory the Great. *The Book of Pastoral Rule*. Translated by Rev. James Barmby, D.D. Edited by Philip Schaff and Henry Wace. *Nicene and Post-Nicene Fathers*, 2nd series, vol. 12. Buffalo, N.Y.: Christian Literature Publishing, 1895.

Groeschel, Benedict. *Spiritual Passages*. New York: Crossroad, 1983.

Hamilton, Edith. *Mythology*. Boston: Little, Brown, 1969.

Hilary of Poitiers. *The Trinity*. Translated by Stephen McKenna, C.Ss.R. The Fathers of the Church, vol. 25. Washington, D.C.: Catholic University of America, 1954.

Hoegerl, Carl, C.Ss.R. *Documentary Study of the Life, Virtues and Reputation for Holiness of the Servant of God Francis X. Seelos, C.Ss.R.* Roma: Tipografia Guerra, 1998.

Hofinger, Johannes, S.J. "How to Pray for Healing". *Priest* 36 (April 1980): 41–46.

Irenaeus. *Against the Heresies*. Translated by Dominic J. Unger, O.F.M. Cap. Ancient Christian Writers, no. 55. New York: Paulist Press, 1992.

————. "Fragments from the Lost Writings of Saint Irenaeus". Edited by Alexander Roberts and James Donaldson. In *Ante-Nicene Fathers*, vol. 1. Buffalo, N.Y.: Christian Literature Publishing, 1885.

John of the Cross. *The Ascent of Mount Carmel*. Translated by David Lewis. London: Thomas Baker, 1922.

————. *The Living Flame of Love*. Translated by David Lewis. London: Thomas Baker, 1919.

John of Damascus. *An Exact Exposition of the Orthodox Faith*. Translated by Stewart Dingwall Fordyce Salmond. Edited by Philip Schaff. Nicene and Post-Nicene Fathers, 2nd series, vol. 9. Buffalo, N.Y.: Christian Literature Publishing, 1899.

John XXIII. *Journal of a Soul*. Translated by Dorothy White. New York: McGraw-Hill, 1965.

John Paul II. *Of the Lay Faithful in the Church and in the World (Christifideles Laici)*. Rome: Libreria Editrice Vaticana, 1988.

————. *On the Holy Spirit in the Life of the Church and the World (Dominum et Vivificantem)*. Rome: Libreria Editrice Vaticana, 1986.

————. *On the Hundredth Anniversary of* Rerum Novarum *(Centesimus Annus)*. Rome: Libreria Editrice Vaticana, 1991.

————. *Redeemer of Man (Redemptor Hominis)*. Rome: Libreria Editrice Vaticana, 1979.

Jones, Frederick M. *Saint Alphonsus Liguori: Saint of Bourbon Naples*. Liguori, Mo.: Liguori Publications, 1992.

Justin Martyr. *Writings of Saint Justin Martyr.* Translated by Thomas B. Falls, D.D., Ph.D. The Fathers of the Church, vol. 6. New York: Christian Heritage, 1948.

Keating, Thomas. *The Heart of the World.* New York: Crossroad, 1981.

Lepp, Ignace. *Death and Its Mysteries.* New York: Macmillan, 1968.

Liguori, Alphonsus Mary de. *Conformity to God's Will.* Translated by Fr. Thomas W. Tobin, C.Ss.R. 1952. Posted on the website of the National Shrine of Saint Alphonsus Liguori, accessed November 17, 2015, http://www.stalphonsusbalt.org/conformity.htm.

—————. *The Great Means of Salvation and of Perfection.* Edited by Rev. Eugene Grimm, C.Ss.R. In *The Complete Works of Saint Alphonsus de Liguori*, vol. 3. Brooklyn, N.Y.: Redemptorist Fathers, 1927.

—————. *Letters.* Edited by Rev. Eugene Grimm. In *The Complete Works of Saint Alphonsus de Liguori*, vol. 1, pt. 1, "General Correspondence". New York: Benziger Brothers, 1891.

—————. *The Passion and the Death of Jesus Christ.* Edited by Rev. Eugene Grimm, C.Ss.R. In *The Complete Works of Saint Alphonsus de Liguori*, vol. 5. Brooklyn, N.Y.: Redemptorist Fathers, 1927.

—————. *The Practice of the Love of Jesus Christ.* Edited by Rev. Eugene Grimm, C.Ss.R. In *The Holy Eucharist*, vol. 6 of *The Complete Ascetical Works of Saint Alphonsus de Liguori*. New York: Benziger Brothers, 1887.

—————. *True Spouse of Jesus Christ.* Edited by Rev. Eugene Grimm, C.Ss.R. In *The Ascetical Works*, vols. 10 and 11 of *The Complete Works of Saint Alphonsus de Liguori*. Brooklyn, N.Y.: Redemptorist Fathers, 1929.

—————. *The Way to Converse Always and Familiarly with God.* Edited by Rev. Eugene Grimm, C.Ss.R. In *The*

Complete Ascetical Works of Saint Alphonsus de Liguori, vol. 2. Brooklyn, N.Y.: Redemporist Fathers, 1926.

————. *The Way of Salvation and Perfection*. Edited by Rev. Eugene Grimm, C.Ss.R. In *The Complete Works of Saint Alphonsus de Liguori*, vol. 2. Brooklyn, N.Y.: Redemptorist Fathers, 1926.

The Liturgy of the Hours. 4 vols. New York: Catholic Book Publishing, 1975, 1976.

McEniry, E. C. *Meditations of Saint Thomas Aquinas, O.P.* Columbus, Ohio: Long's College, 1951.

Merton, Thomas. *The New Man*. New York: Farrar, Straus, and Cudahy, 1961.

————. *New Seeds of Contemplation*. Norfolk, Conn.: New Directions, 1962.

————. *Seeds of Contemplation*. New York: Dell Book, 1949.

————. *The Seven Storey Mountain*. San Diego: Harcourt, Brace, Jovanovich, 1976.

————. *The Waters of Siloe*. New York: Harcourt, Brace, 1949.

New Catholic Encyclopedia. New York: McGraw-Hill, 1967.

Nicolas, Marie Joseph, O.P. *Obedience and the Church*. Washington, D.C.: Corpus Books, 1968.

Nouwen, Henri J. M. *Making All Things New*. San Francisco: Harper and Row, 1981.

Paul VI. *On Evangelization in the Modern World (Evangelii Nuntiandi)*. Rome: Libreria Editrice Vaticana, 1975.

————. *On Fast and Abstinence (Paenitemini)*. Rome: Libreria Editrice Vaticana, 1966.

Payne, Robert. *The Fathers of the Western Church*. London: Heinemann, 1952.

Peck, M. Scott, M.D. *Further Along the Road Less Traveled*. New York: Simon and Schuster, 1993.

Pius XII. *On the Mystical Body of Christ and Our Union in It with Christ (Mystici Corporis Christi)*. June 29, 1943.

Rey-Mermet, Theodule. *St. Alphonsus Liguori: Tireless Worker for the Most Abandoned*. Brooklyn, N.Y.: New City Press, 1987.

Rufino, Mauricio. *A Vademecum of Stories*. New York: Joseph F. Wagner, 1967.

Samra, Cal and Rose. *Holy Humor*. Carmel, N.Y.: Guideposts, 1996.

The Sayings of the Desert Fathers. Translated by Benedicta Ward. London: Mowbrays, 1975.

Sheen, Fulton J. *Treasure in Clay*. San Francisco: Ignatius Press, 1993.

Smith, Gene. "Still Quiet on the Western Front". *American Heritage Magazine* 16, no. 6 (October 1965). www.americanheritage.com/content/still-quiet-western-front.

Spiritual Diary: Selected Sayings and Examples of the Saints. Boston: St. Paul Editions, 1962.

Stevenson, Burton Egbert. *The Macmillan Book of Proverbs, Maxims, and Famous Phrases*. New York: Macmillan, 1948.

The Talmud: Selected Writings. Translated by Ben Zion Bokser. New York: Paulist Press, 1989.

Teresa of Avila. *The Book of Her Life, Spiritual Testimonies, Soliloquies*. Translated by Kieran Kavanaugh, O.C.D., and Otilio Rodriguez, O.C.D. In *The Collected Works of Saint Teresa of Avila*, vol. 1. Washington, D.C.: ICS Publications, 1976.

———. *The Way of Perfection, Meditation on the Song of Songs, The Interior Castle*. Translated by Kieran Kavanaugh, O.C.D., and Otilio Rodriguez, O.C.D. In *The Collected Works of Saint Teresa of Avila*, vol. 2. Washington, D.C.: ICS Publications, 1980.

Thérèse of Lisieux. *Autobiography of St. Thérèse of Lisieux.* Translated by Ronald Knox. New York: P.J. Kenedy and Sons, 1958.

———. *St. Thérèse of Lisieux: Her Last Conversations.* Translated by John Clarke. Washington: ICS Publications, 1977.

Thomas à Kempis. *The Imitation of Christ.* Translated by Aloysius Croft and Harry F. Bolton. Milwaukee: Bruce, 1940.

Vatican II, Dogmatic Constitution on the Church (*Lumen Gentium*). Rome: Libreria Editrice Vaticana, 1964.

Vatican II, Dogmatic Constitution on Divine Revelation (*Dei Verbum*). Rome: Libreria Editrice Vaticana, 1965.

,